UNDERSTANDING THE
PERSON
OF GOD

ELMER L. TOWNS

UNDERSTANDING THE PERSON OF GOD

© Copyright 2020– Elmer L. Towns

All rights reserved. This book is protected by the copyright laws of the United States of America. This book may not be copied or reprinted for commercial gain or profit. The use of short quotations or occasional page copying for personal or group study is permitted and encouraged. Permission will be granted upon request. Unless otherwise identified, Scripture quotations are taken from the New King James Version. Copyright © 1982 by Thomas Nelson, Inc. Used by permission. All rights reserved. Scripture quotations marked BBJ are from the Bible By Jesus®. Copyright © 2018 by Destiny Image and 21st Century Press. All rights reserved. Scripture quotations marked ELT are the author's paraphrases; Elmer L. Towns. Scripture quotations marked KJV are taken from the King James Version. Scripture quotations marked AMP are taken from the Amplified® Bible, Copyright © 2015 by The Lockman Foundation, La Habra, CA 90631. All rights reserved. Used by permission. Scripture quotations marked NIV are taken from the HOLY BIBLE, NEW INTERNATIONAL VERSION®, Copyright © 1973, 1978, 1984, 2011 International Bible Society. Used by permission of Zondervan. All rights reserved. Scripture quotations marked NLT are taken from the Holy Bible, New Living Translation, copyright 1996, 2004, 2015. Used by permission of Tyndale House Publishers., Wheaton, Illinois 60189. All rights reserved. Scripture quotations marked TLB are taken from The Living Bible; Tyndale House, 1997, © 1971 by Tyndale House Publishers, Inc. Used by permission. All rights reserved. Scripture quotations marked NASB are taken from the NEW AMERICAN STANDARD BIBLE®, Copyright © 1960, 1962, 1963, 1968, 1971, 1972, 1973, 1975, 1977, 1995 by The Lockman Foundation. Used by permission. All emphasis within Scripture quotations is the author's own. Please note that Destiny Image's publishing style capitalizes certain pronouns in Scripture that refer to the Father, Son, and Holy Spirit, and may differ from some publishers' styles. Take note that the name satan and related names are not capitalized. We choose not to acknowledge him, even to the point of violating grammatical rules.

DESTINY IMAGE® PUBLISHERS, INC.
P.O. Box 310, Shippensburg, PA 17257-0310
"Promoting Inspired Lives."

This book and all other Destiny Image and Destiny Image Fiction books are available at Christian bookstores and distributors worldwide.

Cover design by Eileen Rockwell

For more information on foreign distributors, call 717-532-3040.

Reach us on the Internet: www.destinyimage.com.

ISBN 13 TP: 978-0-7684-5731-5

ISBN 13 eBook: 978-0-7684-5732-2

For Worldwide Distribution, Printed in the U.S.A.

1 2 3 4 5 6 7 8 / 25 24 23 22 21 20

PAUL EXPLAINS GOD TO UNSAVED GREEKS:

The God I worship...created the world and everything in it...He gives life to everything and everyone...He created one ancestor...the whole human race comes from one man... scattered over the whole face of the earth. God wants all to search for Him so they might find Him.

—Acts 17:23-27 Bible by Jesus

Radical arguments prove and describe the Person of God!

CONTENTS

Preface: God Explains Himself 15

Human Author Explains Himself 19

Section A—Learning My Person-Like Actions: How I Act 23

1   I Am Person—My unlimited power of intellect, emotions, and choice is reflected in self-knowledge and self-direction. 25

2   I Laugh—Salvation of a lost person gives Me joy and laughter. . 29

3   I Sing—I sing to express My joy in your obedience and worship. 33

4   I Smile—I smile on you when you do My will. 37

5   I Whistle—Trust Me to keep My promises, because I will bring Israel back to the Promised Land with a whistle. 41

6   I Read and Write—I keep record in a book that I will read at the Great White Throne Judgment. 45

7   I Whisper—I whisper to get you to stop talking and listen to Me. 48

8	I Walk—I can come to you no matter where you are.	52
9	I Rest—I didn't rest because I was tired, I ceased My creation work on the seventh day.	56
10	I Think—I think about you and know all about you.	59
11	I See—I see everything that can be seen.	62
12	I Cry—Your unbelief in Me brings tears to My eyes.	64

Section B—Learning My Person-Like Reaction: How I Respond . . 69

13	I Frown—Because there are times when I am displeased, you must learn how to approach Me correctly.	71
14	I Get Jealous—You make Me jealous when you put your stuff or another person in My place.	75
15	I Quench (Satisfy)—I want to satisfy the deep longing of people searching for the meaning of life.	79
16	I Think About You—The more you reflect on My purpose for your life, the better you can fulfill My will.	85
17	I Am Sometimes Silent—Sometimes you worship Me best in silent reverence.	89
18	I Have Only Today—Technically, to Me there are no yesterdays or tomorrows, because I am timeless. I live in the "now"!	93
19	I Remember No Longer—Because of My nature, I cannot forget anything, but because of Christ's death, I can choose to forget your sins.	97

20	I Plan—One of the greatest motivations for someone to follow Me, is that I love you and I have a wonderful plan for your life..	101
21	I Choose My Leaders—I choose people to serve Me by looking into their heart.	108
22	I Wait—I do not do everything instantly; I sometimes choose to work slowly through processes of human life.	111
23	I Provide—I provide for My followers the things I promised.	114
24	I Protect—I can protect your health when you live a clean life in My will..	118
25	I Can Be Pleased—I am pleased with the magnitude of your faith and will do great things for you in response to faith.	122
26	I Anguish—To anguish is one of the most desperate emotions, yet I anguish over your sins.	126
27	I Collect Tears in a Bottle—I don't forget about your anguish, so I collect your tears in a bottle.	131
28	I Have Unknowable Secrets—Because you are human, there are certain things about Me you will never know. You must accept and worship Me for what you know about Me.	135
29	I Don't Tell Everything—Because you are human, you couldn't understand all I know, but you must accept and obey what I have told you..	139
30	I Get Angry—You may get angry at the wrong things, at the wrong time; but My anger is always appropriate, because I get angry for the right reasons.	142

31	I Hate Certain Things—I cannot accept what is contrary to or oppose My way of doing things.	146
32	I Punish Sin—Since I have given commandments and principles to serve and please Me, why are you surprised when I punish disobedience?	150

Section C—Learning the Meaning of My Body Parts: My Source of Action **155**

33	I Vomit—I reject things that displease Me or violate My holiness. I expel them from My presence.	157
34	I Turn My Back—No one can see My face and live, but I allowed Moses to see My back side.	160
35	I Have a Face—I tell you to seek My face; and when you find it, you become more like Me.	163
36	I Have a Mind—I want you to understand the reasons why I do the things I do.	168
37	I Have a Heart—You will find My heart when you seek Me wholeheartedly.	173
38	I Have a Nose—I have the ability to appreciate positive/good aromas and reject those smells that are repulsive or obnoxious.	176
39	I Have Eyes—Because I see your sins, you must approach Me with a repentant heart.	180
40	I Have Wax in My Ears—Your sins block your prayers from reaching Me, so that I do not hear your prayers.	183

41   I Use My Fingers—My fingers are an anthropometrism that explains the intricate things I do............................. 187

Section D—Learning My Divine Nature 191

42   I Am Intelligent Designer—Because of My omnipotence, I created a massive universe; and because of My omniscience, I designed the world and humans to live in interaction with the environment. 192

43   I Am the God of Law—My laws are the energy and power by which I run and control the universe..................... 196

44   I Am Unknown, the God of Mystery—You cannot know everything about Me, because as God, I am mystery. So, trust everything you know, and obey all you have learned.......... 204

45   I Am Spirit—Because I am Spirit nature, you cannot see Me, but you can know Me as Person........................ 208

46   I Am Invisible—You cannot see Me or touch Me, but I can see and touch every part of your life. 211

47   I Never Change—You continually change; but you can trust Me, I never change.. 214

Section E—Learning My Absolute Attributes: Omnipotence, Omniscience, Omnipresence 217

48   I Am All-Powerful, Omnipotent—You can trust Me because I can do anything I want to do; nothing is impossible for Me... 218

49   I Am All-Knowing, Omniscient—I know everything possible to know about you and everyone else, and I know everything that has happened, plus everything that has not happened or that could have happened..................................... 222

50 I Am Everywhere All the Time, Omnipresent—You are never alone because I am present everywhere at the same time, all the time. 226

Section F—Learning My Moral Attributes: Love, Holiness, Goodness 231

51 I Am Love—Love is constantly seeing the good in the one thing you love, and then you give yourself for what you love. The essence of love is to focus yourself on the one or the object you love.. 233

52 I Am Holy—Holiness is the essence of purity, and holiness separates itself from sin, wickedness, and rebellion against God. 238

53 I Am Good—The goodness of God is the essence of who God is and what He does. He manifests His nature in the goodness and good things He does. 242

Section G—Learning My Divine Names: God, LORD, Master, Father. 247

54 I Am Elohim, Creator God—The name Elohim means "strong" and reflects the power, majesty, and dominion of God to rule all things.. 249

55 I Am LORD Jehovah, "I AM I AM"—The name LORD means "self-existence" and says, "I Am who I Am.". 258

56 I AM Lord, Adonai, Master—The name Lord means owner, master, or ruler. God is the One who determines what you will do, and He directs your life. He is also the One who determines how you work, assisting in your service to Him.. 263

57   I Am Father—The Father is the Source of life and loving, and with His guidance and help we live for Him.................. 269

Section H—Learning My Trinitarian Nature 273

58   I Am Trinity, Three in One—The Father, Son, and Holy Spirit are equal in divine nature, separate in personal, yet submissive in duties. The Father sent the Son into the world to redeem humanity, and the Father and Son sent the Holy Spirit to deliver salvation to believers and spiritual enablement so they could live and minister victoriously. 275

Afterword 281

About the Author 285

Preface

GOD EXPLAINS HIMSELF

I am the Lord God Almighty, the Creator of the universe. Welcome to the book, *Understanding the Person of God*. The human author is Elmer Towns. He also is the human who translated the Hebrew and Greek Bible into English, *The Bible by Jesus*. But it is not a translation, it is a paraphrase. He translated it into the first person as though Jesus was talking and explaining the Bible.

Now Elmer Towns has written this book in the first person; and in these pages, I am explaining Myself as a Person. I had the traits of personality, long before I created Adam as a human. In the Garden of Eden, I sculptured a clay man—about six feet tall. If you were in the garden at that time you would have seen an unbelievable picture of Me, the eternal God stooping over to breathe My life into that red clay man. I named him Adam, which means *red man*, formed by My hands from the red clay of the Euphrates River. My breath is life—and I breathed Myself into Adam so that he became a living soul...one who would live forever. *Pray: Lord, I am overwhelmed that You breathed Your life into me.*

I made Adam in My image or likeness. He was a person just like Me. But that is not the end of the story, it is the beginning. I put Adam to sleep and took a rib from his side to create a woman—not from his head to be over him, and not from his feet so he would be over her—but from his side to share his life with her.

This first man Adam and his wife, Eve, gave birth to a son, a human creation who came from their physical bodies but made in My image... another person like Me. And what is a person?

A person is someone who knows himself, just as I know Myself—not a surface acquaintance, but knowing himself intimately as only a person knows himself. Just as you know your body parts because they are connected to you, so you know yourself as different from all other people. And then you know yourself intimately from others. *Pray: Lord, teach me who I am and what I am.*

And best of all, you know yourself so you can give direction to yourself. Self-direction based on self-knowledge are the two most powerful forces that makes you human. You are more developed than any other created animals, birds, and water creatures. And you are higher than created plants, grass, air, water, and earth. You—a person—are the ultimate creation, because you are created in My image and likeness.

In the first section of this book I tell you all about My personhood, the last section of this book explains My divine nature and attributes. This last section tells of My creation of time and space. In that section, I also describe My divine attributes: *omniscience,* knowing all things actual and potential at all times; *omnipresence,* being everywhere present equally, at all times; *omnipotence,* being able to do anything I want, in the way I want, at the time I want. All are expressions of My ultimate powerful nature.

The first part of this book is about Me as a person, which is what I want you to focus on first. Because you are a person, I am going to describe Myself in your terminology so you can understand Me with your limited human ability and from your human perspective. *Pray: Lord, teach me more about You.*

God Explains Himself

Because I am Person, I have made you a person—like Me. But you are not unlimited like My divine nature and attributes. No, you are limited. Beginning at birth, you began learning about your personhood, using the facilities of your human personality to learn yourself. But I didn't have to learn about Myself. No! I always knew everything about Myself because I have always existed as God.

So, let's start with your personhood to explain to you who I am. The first forty-one chapters in this book describe Me as Person. Did you know I sing, I wink, I plan, and I weep? You can learn about Me by relating to these characteristics yourself.

The last chapters describe My divine nature and attributes. These descriptions are different from yours. So to understand who I am, how I do what I do, you must think outside your human box. You can learn about Me in the Bible, that is the Book where I reveal who I am and what I do.

The Bible—called the Word of God—is an unusual book. It is not written from theological, doctrinal, encyclopedic, or dictionary perspectives. Rather, I describe Myself by the actions you do, and your reactions to life, and your human thinking. I am like you. That means this book is only a starting place to learn about Me, your heavenly Father.

Being a father, isn't that human? And doesn't a father know his children and love his children and provide for his children? That is who I am and what I do.

This book reaches down to you, a human, to let you know about Me. Remember, I created you as a human, so I know you and understand how you react to life. Also, I sent My Son Jesus Christ to be born a human to live a human life—without sin. As a human, He took your sins and imperfections upon Himself. Since I, the holy God, must punish sin—any sin and all sin—I had to punish Jesus. You have no idea how I felt when My Son cried out from the cross, "My God, My God, why have You forsaken Me" (Matt. 27:46). He didn't call out to Me as His Father, rather He recognized I was the holy God of the universe punishing the sin He had become. *Pray: Lord, thank You for the punishment of Jesus on the cross—for my sins.*

You will learn about My personhood in this book, but there is another purpose. I want you to learn yourself—what makes you tick, what makes you dream, etc. As a human you began learning about yourself and your body needs when you as a baby cried for food, then you ate and drank. Later you learned words, you learned to stand, you learned to walk, you learned your life is a journey of learning how to live and how to adjust.

In this book I want you to learn about Me so you will know yourself better than ever before. Why? Not just to improve your life on earth. I want you to learn how to relate to Me your God, how to serve Me your Master, and how to properly worship Me your LORD and God. *Pray: Lord, as I learn about You, help me know myself better and yield more to You.*

As you read this book listen to your inner person talking to you. Then reach out to learn about Me. You will find I am reaching out to teach you first about Me, then about yourself. *Pray: Lord, I am reaching, amen.*

HUMAN AUTHOR EXPLAINS HIMSELF

I, Elmer L. Towns, have spent my life trying to understand God. This book is an attempt to explain who is God and what does He want of us. It is easy to say God is not an idol carved from stone or made from wood. The "thinking" person knows the vastness of the universe didn't come from a man-made god. The majestic beauty of the world makes you think of a mighty and awesome Creator.

Jesus tells us "God is spirit" (John 4:24), then He directs us to worship Him in Spirit and truth. But even in our worship, it is difficult to worship God wholeheartedly if we do not understand Him completely.

The extreme powerful nature of God can only be partially studied by us humans. It takes an infinite mind to completely understand an infinite God. So, we believe God is omnipotent, omnipresent, and omniscient. But it is hard to get our limited minds around infinity.

The Bible tells us God is love, God is holy, and God is good. Again, we understand with our limited mind the qualities of love, holiness, and goodness. But God is more than infinitely loving or absolute holiness or unquestioned goodness. He is the Source of these moral qualities. Our finite minds cannot understand an infinity of love and holiness and goodness.

UNDERSTANDING THE PERSON OF GOD

How can we begin to understand God?

When you look into a mirror, you see the greatest thing God has conceived or created. What do you see? A normal human with weaknesses, limitations, and failures. Yet how does the Bible describe a human?

> *I am the LORD, your Lord, My name fills the earth.*
> *My glory is seen in the highest heaven.*
> *Look into the night sky to see the work of My fingers.*
> *I set the moon and stars in their places.*
> *Humans can only think about what I have done.*
> *There is nothing they can do about them.*
> *I made people lower than Myself.*
> *Yet I crowned them with glory and honor.*
> *I made people to have dominion over all creation,*
> *Putting all living things under their authority....*
> —Psalm 8:1,3-6, Bible by Jesus

When you begin to understand God, you understand why He created humankind—the highest masterpiece of His creation. But our greatness is not measured in our accomplishments. No! Our greatness is measured by the potential of our Creator.

When you look at the greatness of a human, don't stop there. Look beyond them to their Creator. And to understand the greatness of the Creator, begin by examining the potential of the human who has a small percentage of the potential of their Creator. *Pray: Lord, open my spiritual eyes to see Your potential.*

But this book has taken a new and different path of journalism. Rather than allowing a human author, Elmer Towns, to write and explain his understanding of God, the role is reversed. Elmer Towns writes from the perspective of God. The human will attempt to write and explain how deity—God—would describe Himself. Towns writes this book in the first person as God would write and explain Himself.

Writing in the first person to describe God is not a new experiment to Elmer Towns. He began more than fifteen years ago to translate the Bible from its original Hebrew Old Testament and Greek New Testament into the first person—into the words of Jesus. Towns lets Jesus explain, in English, the Bible from a divine perspective. The end project was named *The Bible by Jesus*, Destiny Image Publishers, Shippensburg, Pennsylvania.

Section A

LEARNING MY PERSON-LIKE ACTIONS: HOW I ACT

The word "anthropomorphism" means ascribing human forms or attributes to deity, animals, or objects.[1] It suggests God can act or do the actions of humans without human physical body parts.

Chapter 1 – I Am Person

Chapter 2 – I Laugh

Chapter 3 – I Sing

Chapter 4 – I Smile

Chapter 5 – I Whistle

Chapter 6 – I Read and Write

Chapter 7 – I Whisper

Chapter 8 – I Walk

Chapter 9 – I Rest

Chapter 10 – I Think

Chapter 11 – I See

Chapter 12 – I Cry

NOTE

1. https://dictionary.cambridge.org/dictionary/english/anthropomorphism; accessed June 7, 2020.

1

I AM PERSON

> *Christ is the brightness of the Father's glory and the perfect image of His person....* —Hebrews 1:3 ELT
>
> *So God created man in His own image; in the image of God He created him; male and female He created them.* —Genesis 1:27
>
> *And the LORD God formed man of the dust of the ground and breathed into his nostrils the breath of life; and man became a living being.* —Genesis 2:7

Most religions of the world reflect Me as a distant, uninterested power or just a force. Some see Me as an impersonal being, just as a plate on a table or a picture on the wall. Others say I am just an idea. But these designations all fall way short of My New Testament description. So, who am I? To understand Me, look at the pinnacle of My creation, look at Adam. Because I created Adam like Me, I am person. *Pray: Lord, open My spiritual eyes to see You.*

Can you get to know Me? Zophar, the friend of Job asked, "Canst thou by searching find out God?" (Job 11:7 KJV). The answer is yes! But you must come to Me on My terms. Jeremiah 29:13 says, "You will seek Me and find Me, when you seek Me with all your heart." You can know

Me and you can learn about Me through My personality with functions and properties as seen in human personalities.

For example, you can talk to Me in prayer as you talk to other people, because I have all the properties of a person to hear and talk. In other words, I have the power of personality. I am not a person because you project onto Me your power of personality. The opposite is true; you get your personality from Me because I was originally person.

In the beginning in the garden, We the Trinity talked together and said, "Let Us make man in Our image" (Gen. 1:26). When you see yourself in the mirror each morning, what do you see? You see an exact reflection or image of yourself. But when I look into your face, I see an image of Myself. Not physically, but I see you as a person who can think, feel, and make decisions, just as I can. You are self-identifying and self-directing, just as I am. Of course, your characteristics are much more finite while My characteristics of personality are infinite. *Pray: Lord, look into my heart to see my love for You.*

I am wise in creation (see Prov. 3:14), wise in preserving life (see Neh. 9:6), wise in My providence (see Eph. 1:11), and wise in redemption (see Eph. 1:7). Since intelligence is essential to personality and I am infinite, you must conclude that I have infinite intelligence.

I have a mind (see Gen. 18:19; Exod. 3:7). I remember (see Gen. 8:1). I reason (see Isa. 1:18). Speech is based on your recall of word symbols, and I do that. And because I have a mind to think, I have created rationality in you. Now I expect you to think your thought after My example or pattern. *Pray: Lord, I will fill my mind with Scriptures to think properly.*

I have emotions, so I created the passion of life in you. You love your mother, pizza, and your free time. I love (see John 3:16), am kind (see Ps. 103:8-13), I empathize with people (see Exod. 3:7-8), I feel sorrow (see John 11:35), I grieve (see Gen. 6:6), and I get angry at evil (see Ps. 7:11). Yet of all My emotions, My love is most powerful and best known. I love perfectly because I am perfect. I love because of My nature; that is who I am. *Pray: Lord, thank You for loving me.*

The ultimate act of personality is the ability to make decisions that give direction to your life. I have the power of volition, which means I have the freedom and ability to make decisions, so I created into you the ability to make choices and to direct your life by good decisions. At times I make decisions based on what I know; and at other times, I choose out of My love or My hatred for sin and disobedience. Still at other times, I make decisions out of My volitional nature. However, since I am a person, I act as a unit. Therefore, My will is the natural extension of what I think, feel, and desire.

I am a person with self-perception or the power to know Myself. I told Moses, "I AM THAT I AM" (Exod. 3:14 KJV), which means I have self-awareness. I am aware of who I am and I am aware of what I can do.

When I told Moses, "I will certainly be with you" (Exod. 3:12), I was exercising self-direction. Thousands of times throughout Scripture I have said "I will" meaning I have self-determination. I am free to do what I choose.

All of these aspects demonstrate that I have personality. I have a mind to think, emotions to feel deeply, and volition to choose to do My will. I have self-perception and self-direction.

MY CHOICE

I can do whatever I choose to do.
I have not chosen to do everything.
When I choose to do anything, nothing can stop Me.
I choose at times not to do everything I can do.
I honor free will and I have given people their free will.

Some ask the question, "Can you rightly call Me—God—a person?" That's an excellent question because the word "person" is so small and limiting. You think of those you know with personality, and you think of a winsome personality or a belligerent personality. To you, personality is such a limiting word. But I am so much greater than personality. To think of Me is to think of mysteries, majesty, and power. Yes, I am a person, it is the very core of who I am, but I am much greater and much more majestic. I am God!

YOUR TIME TO PRAY

Lord, I come to You, knowing You hear me when I pray,
You love me because of Your nature,
You have chosen a plan for my life.
Lord, I come worshipping You and praising Your name,
You have done so much for me.
But the greatest thing is that you know me intimately;
God, You let me know You in return.
Lord, I reach out to touch You with my worship,
But more importantly, touch me with Your presence.
Amen.

2

I LAUGH

> *Likewise, I (Jesus) say unto you, My Father gets happy in heaven in the presence of His angels when one lost sinner repents.* —Luke 15:10 ELT

"Do you hear that," a man asked cupping his hand behind his ear. "I'd recognize that laugh anywhere." He was standing at the opening into a valley but couldn't see into the valley because it was night. The voice coming toward him from the valley was not yelling for help. It was laughing.

The valley was desolate, a place no one would visit after dark. There were steep rocks and dangerous pits. If you fell in one, there was no escape. Black openings to threatening caves concealed unknown hungry predators lurking within.

"Listen," the man said, "you can hear a voice clearly…and it's a happy voice."

Walking up the valley came a shepherd with a sheep on his shoulder. His laughter was infectious; you wanted to laugh with him. "Rejoice with me, I have found my sheep."

At sundown the shepherd had been tired from chasing stray sheep in the hot sun. He was looking forward to a hot meal and the rest of sleep.

But he didn't eat first. He constantly circled his flock looking for snakes, alkaline water, or poisonous roots. His sheep were gullible; they had no sense of danger.

As the sun was setting the shepherd began a small fire to cook a simple meal and rest. "Soon I can sleep," he thought. He called his sheep by name, and most obeyed to enter the sheepfold. Then the shepherd called a name of a rebellious sheep, one that had difficulty obeying.

No movement in the flock; no response. The sheep didn't come.

The shepherd circled the flock again, looking for any telltale evidence of the rebellious one. The rebellious sheep could not be seen. With panic the shepherd rapidly gathered all the flock into the sheepfold. It was a rock wall enclosure that was overgrown with thorns and thistles—to keep sheep in and predators out.

The shepherd called the name again, but no answer. Then he carefully counted...97...98...99... one missing.

The shepherd would never say, "Serves him right for running away!" Nor would the shepherd eat his hot meal and get some needed sleep. No! He left his other sheep locked safely in their pen to go searching immediately for his lost sheep. A good shepherd would sacrifice his comfort, not thinking of his tired body. He would face the dangers of the night to find one lost sheep. Why would he do that? Love! Shepherds love their sheep.

I, Jesus told this parable of the Lost Sheep in Matthew 18:12-14 and Luke 15:3-7. My listeners, many of whom might have been shepherds themselves, would have understood the imagery and the point I was making. Today, few people are familiar with shepherding, so the depiction might be a bit tougher for you to grasp. But all can understand the sacrifices a mother makes for her baby. All have seen a pet owner cry when burying their beloved dog or cat. All can understand love.

I love sinners and have gone to unfathomable lengths to rescue them. Angels worshipped Me and do My bidding in heaven, but I gave up the comforts of heaven to come to earth. I came not to be served, but to serve and sacrifice My life as a ransom for all. I came seeking lost sheep. *Pray: Thank You, Jesus, for coming to find me.*

Because I lived a perfect life without sin, men who were sinners hated Me, ridiculed Me, and condemned Me to death. They crushed a crown of thorns on My head and beat Me viciously with a cat-o'-nine-tails whip. When I had no strength left, they forced Me to carry a cross—the instrument of execution—up a hill called Calvary. They laid Me upon that cross and drove spikes through My hands and feet. They stood the cross in the blazing sun and left Me to die.

I your Shepherd died for you and the sheep of this world. Why? Because I love them. Because they were lost. Because they couldn't help themselves. *Pray: Lord, I bow in utter amazement.*

The sheep of this world are gullible; they have no sense of danger. They eat, sleep, and do the things they want to do, not realizing how close danger lurks. Why did I die for this adrift bunch? Because I love them.

Listen to My laughter! As I the Shepherd come with another sheep I have rescued. I am laughing as I carry the sheep on My shoulder. Listen as I shout to the other sheep, "Rejoice with Me for I have found My sheep which was lost" (Luke 15:6 ELT).

Why do I laugh? The salvation of a lost person makes Me happy. There is not much in the Bible that describes My laughing except My rejoicing over lost people being saved: "Likewise I (Jesus) say to you, 'The Father gets happy in heaven in the presence of His angels over one lost sinner that repents'" (Luke 15:10 ELT).

What makes you happy in this life? And with whom do you celebrate when you are happiest? If you get a pay raise, do you celebrate with fellow workers? With your spouse? With a best friend? Apparently, I celebrate with the angels. *Pray: Lord, thank You for rejoicing over me in front of the angels.*

You can tell a lot about a person by what makes them happy. Since you are made in My image, you should have the same likes and dislikes as I have. Winning souls makes Me happier than anything else because creating man was greater to Me than creating the universe. Creation was the greatest thing I did until My birth as the Christ child to a virgin in Bethlehem. Greater yet was My dying on the cross for humankind—and greater than that was My being raised from the dead to give life.

No wonder I laugh with enjoyment when someone is saved!

YOUR TIME TO PRAY

Lord, thank You for coming to seek me, a lost sheep;
Thank You for seeking me when I was lost.
Thank You for rescuing me from sin's danger,
And giving me salvation from sin.
Lord, I rejoice with You for the Bible says, "You laugh"
When someone is saved.
I laugh with You because I was one who was saved.
I was lost but now I am found.
Amen.

3

I SING

> *For I the LORD your God has arrived to live among you. I am a mighty Savior. I will rejoice over you in great gladness; I will love you and not accuse you. Do you hear that joyous choir? No, it is Me, your LORD Myself rejoicing over you in happy song.* —Zephaniah 3:17 BBJ

Charles Billingsley, the famous contemporary gospel soloist, has been asked many times if he sings to his wife. The truth is...he does not—she hears him enough at church and in concerts. But when their two boys were little, he would sing to them every night. It seemed to comfort them and help them relax. Then Charles asked himself if I the Lord loves to sing over My people just as he (Charles), loves to sing over his children.

Can you imagine Me the Lord singing? Do you think I am a tenor, bass, or baritone? What kind of songs would I sing? When would I sing? What would motivate Me to sing? When humans think of all the reasons why they sing, it helps to realize why I your Lord would sing.

Sometimes, you sing when you are happy. Children on the way to camp sing "camp songs" because they anticipate a week of fun, adventure, and getting away from home. They sing with laughter and anticipation. Do you think I sing with laughter and anticipation over what humans are going to do for Me?

Some sing because they are in love. Picture a young girl with her first boyfriend. She feels as though she is running through a flowery meadow on a bright sunny day. Her feet barely touch the ground. She is singing on perfect pitch. Her songs represent pure joy, anticipation of marriage and the happiness she will have with the man of her dreams. Do you think that I your Lord sing a love song in anticipation of His love-relationship with you?

Then again, other people sing because of their sadness, and their music is a wail that expresses the sorrows and trials of life. Think of the old spiritual composed in slavery, "Nobody Knows de Trouble I Seen." While bound in chains, the slaves sang out of hope for better days to come. They sang about their troubles and the anticipation of meeting Me their Lord in death. Do you think I your Lord sing a sad song because of your bondage to sin, or your obedience to satan?

Other times a song can express a story or drama, such as Broadway musicals or the classic operas. Some sing a song about their work, while others sing a song of relaxation like "Macarena" or "Take Me Out to the Ballgame." In each of these songs, you tell what you are doing or the things you want to do. Do you think I your Lord will sing over you as you carry out My work of salvation in your life?

Sometimes you sing patriotic songs to stir your devotion to your country or cause. You sing "The National Anthem" to invoke your loyalty to your nation, or you pledge your allegiance with singing. Sometimes your song declares that you will fight for your country. Patriotic music stirs your allegiance and makes your feet want to march. Do you think I your Lord sing to get you to pledge your allegiance to the Kingdom of heaven?

There are times when you sing a lullaby to put a baby to sleep. Your singing puts everything out of your infant's mind so the child will rest and drift into sleep. You sing softly and melodically to soothe a baby crying. Do you think I sing a lullaby over you to soothe away your hurts and fears?

I Sing

Sometimes you sing because you are full of joy and happiness. At a birthday party, you join in singing "Happy Birthday." At other times, people sing to communicate a message.

Christians sing evangelistic songs to motivate people to get saved or missionary songs to challenge people to carry out the Great Commission. Do you think I sing because I have a message I want you to give out?

Notice what the Bible says about My singing: "The LORD Himself (is) singing over you in happy song" (Zeph. 3:17 ELT). This verse tells you that I rejoice over you, so I sing because you have done something to make Me rejoice. *Pray: Lord, I want to make You happy.*

Have you ever thought that you could make Me, your Lord happy? I rejoice when you keep My commandments wholeheartedly. *Pray: Lord, make me obedient.*

Many verses in the Bible tell you to rejoice in Me, your Lord. But there are a few occasions that tell you I your God rejoice (see Ps. 60:6). I rejoice when you are married to Me in salvation, just as a bride rejoices in her coming marriage (see Isa. 62:5). Also, I get pleasure out of My creations: "I your LORD shall rejoice in My works" (Ps. 104:31 BBJ).

Deuteronomy 30 tells of the curses I put upon My people for disobeying Me. But I rejoice if they will "again obey My voice and do all My commandments" (Deut. 30:8 BBJ). "I will restore My blessings; their farms will prosper, and they will enjoy the fruit of their labor. But most of all, I their LORD will again rejoice over them for good" (Deut. 30:9 BBJ). I am happy when My children repent and come back to Me.

When someone praises Me their Lord, do I rejoice with them? When they "sing praises to Me" (Ps. 149:3), what happens? The Bible says, "Because I take pleasure in My people" (Ps. 149:4 BBJ). So, when people sing and rejoice, I take pleasure in them, and I sing over them. *Pray: Lord, I sing to You, and I want you to sing over me.*

There is a relationship between My joy and your joy. I give you My joy when you obey My Word. When that happens, you have My joy filling your heart. Jesus said, "These things have I spoken unto you that My joy might remain in you and that your joy may be full" (John 15:11 KJV). *Pray: Lord, fill me with Your joy.*

So, do not think your happiness originates in you. Do not think you are the one who makes others happy. No, you must remember you are made in My image and you get good things from Me. Your only real joy or happiness comes from Me. It is only natural for Me to be happy, so when you rejoice, you are expressing My joy that I your Lord have given you. So, sing joyfully to Me because I am singing over you.

YOUR TIME TO PRAY

Lord, it thrills me to know You rejoice over me,
And You rejoice over me in singing.
May I always obey Your commandments
And seek Your presence in worship.
May I give You many reasons to sing over me.
Lord, I know You are the Source of rejoicing and happiness.
I live in You because I have a new nature.
I will sing because joy comes from Your presence.
Amen.

4

I SMILE

> *May I your LORD bless you and protect you. May I your LORD smile on you and be gracious to you. May I your LORD show you My favor and give you My peace.*
> —Numbers 6:24-26 ELT

A man and wife had been studying the Mona Lisa for a long time, neither one saying much. The world-famous painting of Mona Lisa by Leonardo DaVinci hung in the Louvre in Paris, France, had been one of the special works of art they wanted to see on their trip to Europe.

"What do you admire most?" the husband asked.

"The mix of colors and shadowing," answered the wife. "I can't tell if Leonardo painted early morning or late evening."

"Why is this a world-famous painting?" the husband again asked.

"The woman in the painting has alluring features, although she's not especially beautiful," the wife answered. Then she added, "We can't tell much about her. There's so much mystery in the painting."

The man looked at the painting from the left, and then from the right. He wanted to see if different light on the Mona Lisa solved some of the mystery. Then his face lit up as if he had found the secret to Mona

UNDERSTANDING THE PERSON OF GOD

Lisa. "I can't tell if she's smiling or not!" Before his wife could answer the husband continued, "I can't tell what she's smiling about."

A smile communicates many messages. The Mona Lisa smile could express a timid shyness or an irritating smugness. She could be saintly or regretful. calm and confident, tentative and unsure about what she's going to do. She could be cynical or rueful. The Mona Lisa is world famous not because of what we know about her smile—but because of what we don't know. We don't know why she smiles!

Did you know that I your Lord smile?

Why do I smile and when do I smile? Have I ever smiled on you? Would you like Me to smile on you today?

Webster's dictionary has several definitions for the word "smile." First, "to wonder" or "to be caught by surprise." Yes, I smile but I never am surprised because I know all things, at all times, both actual and potential.

The second part of the definition is "to look or regard with amusement or ridicule." Again, this is not the reason I smile. I didn't create you for My amusement, nor to ridicule you.

The third part of the definition is, "to approve or express happiness."[1] This is why I smile.

What makes Me happy? When you approach Me your heavenly Father through the blood of My Son, I accept you in grace. When you completely yield your selfish plans and projects to Me, I take you into My care. When you attempt to serve Me with all your heart, mind, and strength, saying, "Not I, but Christ," I embrace you. When you seek to know Me intimately, saying, "You my Lord are all I need," then I smile. *Pray: Lord, I love Your smile.*

When I smile, you know I am happy with you. Isn't a smile one of the greatest experiences that a person can have? And the greatest they can give? Greater than the pleasure of receiving any gift, greater than any reward or greater than any promotion, a smile reflects your oneness with another person. To know Me personally and to realize that I accept you and I am happy with you—because I smile at you—is the greatest thing in life. *Pray: Lord, I look forward to Your daily smile.*

The priestly benediction at the beginning of this chapter was pronounced by a priest when dismissing a worshipper who had come to bring a gift or sacrifice to Me. The person has supposedly come with the right attitude and had brought the right sacrifice to the right place. The priest offers the gift to Me for the worshipper, and then to conclude the worship experience, he pronounces this benediction that includes, "May the LORD's face smile upon you" (see Num. 6:25).

If you want My blessing, make sure your heart has the right attitude when you approach Me. Make sure you've done the right thing and approach Me in the right way. *Pray: Lord, teach me how to properly approach You.*

Some don't know how to approach Me, so they don't enjoy My smile, just as a child doesn't get a parent's smile when they are mischievous or rebellious. What about a spouse? You don't get a smile when you knowingly do something your spouse doesn't like. A smile from your spouse makes life easier. It's what marriage is all about!

What about My smile? Isn't My smile what Christianity is all about?

YOUR TIME TO PRAY

Lord, when I heard that You smile,
It made me realize that You love me, and I can please You.
Lord, teach me how to reach Your heart,
And give me the passion to love You with all my heart.
Lord, I yield all of myself to You this day;
I seek You with all of my heart,
Smile on me and be gracious to me, give me Your peace.
Amen.

NOTE

1. Webster's New Collegiate Dictionary (Springfield, MA: Merriam-Webster Inc., 1976), s.v. "smile."

5

I WHISTLE

> *I raise a signal flag for the distant nations; and whistle for them from the ends of the earth. Look—how quickly and swiftly they come!* —Isaiah 5:26 ELT

Elmer Towns and his wife, Ruth, fell in love at Columbia Bible College in the early 1950s. The school had rules for couples going steady that prevented them from spending too much time together. They were allowed two dates a week, and they could talk briefly in the halls between classes. But there was no endless hanging out like young couples are prone to do today.

Elmer worked in the school kitchen in a variety of jobs. One was breakfast setup, which included putting out milk, juice, cereals, and making coffee.

Ruth lived on the fourth floor of the women's dorm; her window was right over the door where Elmer entered the kitchen every morning.

He arrived each morning around 5:45 a.m. Usually everything was quiet. No street noise and no activity in the dorms. When he approached the dorm, he would whistle "I Dream of Jeanie with the Light Brown Hair." The light would go on, the shades would roll up and there she was at the window waving at him. Her middle name was Jean.

Elmer's morning whistle was a signal to her, which allowed them a few more seconds of interaction each day. Even though they couldn't talk, that was a special time together. Elmer could feel his emotions running as he got close to the kitchen door.

A whistle was his signal.

In Wild West movies, the hero would signal for his horse to come to him with a whistle. A boy whistles for his dog the same way. Construction workers whistle a signal to one another. And don't you whistle your approval for a home run, touchdown or winning basket?

Elmer's mother used to whistle for him when he was out playing in the neighborhood. Along about sundown she would come to the back porch, lean over the banister toward the place where he was playing, put her fingers in her mouth and whistle the loudest signal in our neighborhood. Our neighborhood was two blocks across and five blocks long, so he could hear her anywhere he was playing.

Her whistle was an invitation, a signal that supper was on the table. He always came running when she called because the food she had on the table was better than any game Elmer could play. There was always a home-cooked meal waiting: meat, potatoes, three or four vegetables out of the garden, and a big glass of iced tea, already sweetened. This was his mother's happiest time of day because she loved to see her family enjoy the meal, almost as much as she enjoyed cooking it.

Did you know that I whistled when I wanted to signal Israel to come home? One day in the future, I will go out on the back porch of heaven, lean over the banister of paradise and whistle for My children—Israel—to come home to the Promised Land. From all around the world the Jews will return to the land that will flow with milk and honey. "He will lift up a flag to [call] the distant nations [to bring His judgment on Judah], and will whistle for them [His people] from the ends of the earth; and indeed, they will come with great speed swiftly"

(Isa. 5:26 AMP). And what son of Abraham could stay away when I whistle for them to come home?

And when they return, look at the smile on My Father's face. And just like Elmer's mother, who reveled in people eating her home cooking almost as much as preparing the meal, the Father will have fulfilled His promises. He will smile as His people Israel come home to supper.

My whistle tells you three things. First, I keep My Word. I made a promise to Abraham (see Gen. 12:7), Isaac (see Gen. 26:3) and Jacob (see Gen. 35:12) that I would give the land of Israel to their descendants. My whistle signals that I am keeping My promise and giving them the Promised Land.

Second, I am whistling for My people to come home to rest and have peace. For thousands of years the Jews have been persecuted; but when I whistle for them, they will be coming home to peace.

Third, My whistle means it's the end. Just as Elmer's mother whistled for him to stop playing and come home at the end of a day, so I whistle at the end of the Dispensation of the Gentiles. My whistle begins the Millennial Age for the Jews.

But you saved Gentiles are not waiting for a whistle. You are waiting for a shout from heaven. It will be Me calling you to meet Me in the air: "For I the Lord shall descend from heaven with a shout...and My physically dead ones will rise first. Then those who are alive and remain shall be caught up together with them in the clouds to meet Me their Lord in the air; and so shall we ever be with Me" (1 Thess. 4:16-17 ELT).

Honestly do you care what you hear? Whether it's a whistle or a shout, you are looking for a Person. You are waiting for Me, the Lord Jesus. *Pray: Lord, I'm listening.*

YOUR TIME TO PRAY

Lord, a whistle can be a good thing.
I whistle when I'm glad or amazed.
I whistle my joy and worship to You.
Lord, be blessed with my worship that comes from my heart.
Be pleased when I worship You sincerely.
Amen.

6

I READ AND WRITE

> *And John the apostle saw Me the Lord, sitting on the Great White Judgment Throne...and the dead stood before Me to be judged. The books of works were opened where I sentenced the dead according to their works. Then the Lamb's Book of Life was opened and anyone whose name was not written there was cast into the Lake of Fire.*
>
> —Revelation 20:11-15 ELT

Did you know that I your God have a record of all your works? Does that mean I write because there is a record of all you do? Does it mean that I can read?

In times past, people wrote by hand. Does that mean I wrote your record by hand? Am I up-to-date? Do you think I now keep My records on a computer? Maybe a laptop? That would mean I have learned to type. By the time you update your thinking about My records, maybe I will keep them on a smart phone, an iPad, or maybe I will use a device that is not yet invented.

Of course, I am not limited by time. My Son Jesus is yesterday, today, and forever. Maybe I used a upgraded computer before computers were invented. Just as a computer contains written files, perhaps a voice-activated computer of the future could have My records.

Have you ever thought that I do not need to write things down? I know all things perfectly from the beginning. I know without effort. In fact, if I had to write things down to remember them, that means at a past time, I did not know everything because I had to give effort to know them. That meant I was not Godlike—but I AM God.

I do not write down things for My benefit. I keep records for your benefit. I write things down and reveal them to you for your sake.

When I judge the unsaved, they can never say I am bias, because their record speaks for itself. The unsaved can never say I make mistakes, because the record is accurate. The unsaved can never say someone changed his or her record. Their record is complete, true, and permanent. Finally, the unsaved cannot say that I did not know what they were doing. My record includes both motives and actions. The Bible says, "people are without excuse" (Rom. 1:20 NIV). *Pray: Lord, I know my name is written in the Lamb's Book of Life.*

Do not forget that I also keep records to reward My children. I give a crown of rejoicing for those who win the lost to salvation (see 1 Thess. 2:19-20; Phil. 4:1). Those who bravely endure persecution for My sake will receive a crown of life (see Rev. 2:10). Those who practice self-discipline will receive an incorruptible crown (see 1 Cor. 9:25). Those who teach and shepherd others will receive the crown of glory (see 1 Peter 5:1-4), and finally, there is a crown of righteousness for those who love My appearing (see 2 Tim. 4:8). *Pray: Lord, it is not a crown I seek; I just want to be with You in heaven.*

Receiving crowns will not be like a military service where men and women are given ribbons to wear proudly. When you appear before My throne, you will see that you were not responsible for everything you did that deserves merit. No! I did it through you. My Son, Jesus Christ deserves your rewards. You will see your unworthiness when you see My face. The Bible describes that you will cast your crowns before the throne (Rev. 4:10). *Pray: Lord, I give all my rewards to You.*

I see all you do, and I write a record in My book. Then when you appear before My throne, I will have something good to say about you, and every other one of My children. No matter how little you have done, I will have a reward for you. Because I care about everyone, I know what each has done. The Bible promises, "Then each man will receive praise from Me" (1 Cor. 4:5 ELT).

YOUR TIME TO PRAY

Lord, I read in Your Word you've forgiven all my sins,
"The blood of Jesus Christ His Son
Cleanses me from all sin" (1 John 1:7).
So I will not appear at the Great White Judgment Throne
Only the unsaved will be there to be judged out of Your books.
Lord, You wrote my name in the Lamb's Book of Life
Then You read my name written there
Thank You for saving me from the Lake of Fire.
Amen.

7

I WHISPER

> *I the Lord told Elijah, "Go out and stand before Me on the mountain. And as Elijah stood there, I the Lord passed by, and a mighty windstorm hit the mountain. It was such a terrible blast that the rocks were torn loose, but I the Lord was not in the wind. After the wind there was an earthquake, but I the Lord was not in the earthquake. And after the earthquake there was a fire, but I the Lord was not in the fire. And after the fire there was the sound of a gentle whisper".* —1 Kings 19:11-12 ELT

Elmer Towns married a gentle woman. His wife, Ruth, had never raised her voice or yelled at him. For the longest time, he did not realize how fortunate he was until he became a pastor and got involved in counseling married couples through their knockdown, drawn-out fights. He saw women lose their temper and their feminine softness. They yelled at their husband and poured out their "hurt" in moments of uncontrollable rage.

Elmer soon realized how blessed he was. Ruth did not yell for the kids when she wanted them to come, nor did she raise her voice at them in anger or frustration. She also did not yell at him, though sometimes she would quietly write him notes to tell how she felt. She did not tell

I Whisper

him he was wrong, for that was not her style, but she wanted him to know how she felt about things.

She whispered!

So how did she make the kids do right? She did not have to yell because the kids knew what she wanted them to do. They could see it in her face or feel it in the atmosphere. Maybe it was the Holy Spirit speaking to them. The kids always knew their mother did not yell, but they all said, "Watch out when she whispers!"

When people yell at each other, two things happen. First, both turn up the volume to out-yell the other. Second, the more they yell, the less they listen. Don't you think I know that?

So I seldom yell to get your attention. If I yelled at people, instead of listening, they would yell right back.

I know people stop listening to those who yell at them. So, when I want you to listen to Me, what do I do?

I whisper!

Look at the verse again; I, Elijah's God came to him with a still small voice. A whisper is the opposite of loud, bold Elijah. How loud was Elijah? Once he gathered almost a 1,000 prophets of Baal on Mount Carmel for a religious shout-out. Can you hear him yelling a challenge to 950 ungodly prophets? "THE GOD WHO ANSWERS BY FIRE, HE IS GOD" (1 Kings 18:24).

They had a contest to see who could bring fire from heaven. The prophets of Baal went first. They placed their sacrifice on the altar and cried aloud, "O BAAL, HEAR US!" (1 Kings 18:26). But Baal did not exist—except in name—so he didn't answer.

Sarcastically Elijah prodded them, "Cry aloud...either he is meditating, or he is busy...or perhaps he is sleeping and must be awakened" (1 Kings 18:27). But yelling didn't get an answer from Baal.

Then Elijah prayed, and I answered from heaven with fire. Elijah commanded the crowd, "Seize the prophets of Baal! Do not let one of them escape!" (1 Kings 18:40). The false prophets were executed. In revenge, Queen Jezebel swore she would have Elijah's head. The bold prophet Elijah ran across the nation Israel, then across Judah, and into the desert where he prayed to die. The spectacular events on Mount Carmel were not enough to convince Elijah to continue his ministry.

Elijah continued running away. He left the Holy Land and crossed the desert, traveling all the way south to the Sinai Peninsula. Was Elijah running from Jezebel? Was Elijah running from his perceived inadequacies? Was Elijah running from Me?

Maybe Elijah was running from My call upon his life. When he got to Mount Sinai, he complained to Me that he was a failure, saying, "I alone am left; and they seek to take my life" (1 Kings 19:10).

Notice, I did not run after Elijah, nor did I yell to get the prophet's attention. I let Elijah feel the loneliness of his failure. When Elijah was left frustrated and at the end of his rope, then he was ready to listen to Me.

I came to Elijah, but not in a mighty hurricane, not in an earthquake, and not in a consuming fire. I did not need noise or force. I already had Elijah's attention. So I whispered.

Why do I whisper? I your God whisper because I want your attention. No one likes to be yelled at, and you often reject anyone who yells at you, or you end up yelling back. *Pray: Lord, You have my attention. Speak...I will listen to You.*

Why do I whisper? Because those who yell blur their words and phrases. You hear noise, but you miss the message. I do not want you to miss My message, so I whisper. *Pray: Lord, I do not want to miss Your message to me.*

Why do I whisper? Because you get quiet when someone whispers to you. You usually stop what you are doing and focus all your physical attention on the whisperer so you can hear what is being said. Isn't that why I whisper? I want you to stop doing what you are doing—whether you are sinning or going about your business—I whisper so you will stop and focus on Me. *Pray: Lord, I have stopped. Help me to be still so I can listen to You.*

Why do I whisper? To get you to listen attentively to Me. When I whisper, you focus on My message and Me. *Pray: Lord, when You whisper, I will make You the focus of my life and service.*

YOUR TIME TO PRAY

*Lord, You whispered to get Elijah's attention,
And You speak to me quietly in the blackness of night.
I want to hear and know what You say.
Lord, You speak quietly in my heart so I won't miss Your message;
Help me understand what You want me to do.
I will obey Your silent words and do what You tell me.
I will be Your servant.
Amen.*

8

I WALK

> *And they [Adam and Eve] heard the sound of the LORD God walking in the garden in the cool of the day....*
> —Genesis 3:8
>
> *I will walk among you and be your God, and you shall be My people.* —Leviticus 26:12
>
> *For the LORD your God walks in the midst of your camp, to deliver you...therefore, your camp shall be holy, that He may see no unclean thing among you, and turn away from you.* —Deuteronomy 23:14

I, the Lord God, am Spirit (John 4:24), and a spirit does not have legs to walk. But I walk—your Lord and Creator God walk. No, I don't have legs, but just as you move from one place to another on legs, I move from one place to another, not on legs, but I nevertheless move.

Let's look at the dictionary definition of "walk." First, it is moving at a regular pace, lifting and setting one's foot in front of the other to move the body. While that is true, the dictionary has a second definition: to guide, accompany, or escort (someone) on foot. A third definition is broader: to follow a teaching, set of principles, many directions as an illustration, "walking in fear of the Lord."

But I your Lord and Master walk in the sense of the first and second definition—I move from one location to another. I walked to protect the people of Israel when they were in the wilderness, much as a sentry or night guard walks to protect or secure a location he is guarding.

The sound of My voice was walking in the Garden of Eden. Notice, it was not My legs, but the sound of My voice walking. I was not looking for Adam, I know where all people are located at all times, at all places in My universes. So, I knew Adam and Eve were hiding from Me. I also know they heard My walking, because I know all sounds made in every place in My universes at all times.

I could have gone searching for Adam without making a sound. I could have been silent, but they heard Me walking. When I called out, "Where are you?" (Gen. 3:9), I was not asking for My benefit. I knew where they were located, I yelled for their benefit. It was My first move to convict them of their sin. After all, isn't conviction defined "to cause to see?" Yes! I was causing them to see their sin as I see sin.

But there are other reasons why I walk. When I walked among the tribes of Israel as they wander in the desert, I was protecting them. And how did I protect Israel? Many ways. First, I was the Shekinah Glory Cloud that could been seen by any hostile tribe or group that might attack Israel. But also, I was there in My localized presence. If any attacked My people, I could rally them to fight, energize them to fight, or I could defeat any enemy fighting against Israel. *Pray: Lord, protect me in ways I don't pray.*

But there was another feature about My walking in and through Israel's campground. I gave them peace and security, so they felt protected when I walked in their midst. Would you feel protected if you knew I was walking with you?

There are many ways to walk. You can hike, jaunt, parade, stroll, march, tramp, trod, or perambulate. When you think of all the ways you walk, remember when you say, "God walks" that it is a figure of speech or as theologians call it an *anthropomorphism*. That word means, My actions are described as human functions or acts. Therefore, I go from one place to another in many different ways. Don't get lost in the figure of speech when you try to project into your limited human life such metaphors as My walking.

There is another problem with My walking. What about My omnipresence. I am everywhere equally present at the same time, all the time. How could I walk from one location to another, or move from one location to another, if I am already present at all places. Think of My localized presence, meaning I personify Myself at one place by manifesting Myself and My characteristics. This is also called My manifest presence because at that place I choose to manifest Myself. So, when I walk from one place to another, I may choose to manifest Myself in one place, then I manifest Myself in movement. Finally, I manifest Myself as I arrive at My destination. *Pray: Lord, walk close to me so I realize Your presence.*

So, walking doesn't describe Me from My point of view. It is for you and all other humans to focus your attention on Me and My manifestation of Myself as I go from one location to another. Walking is a limited term to describe or limit activity that you do with your limited understanding of time, space, and reality. So, when I describe Myself walking, it is to help you understand something about Me, even when you or any human cannot understand all things about Me.

I Walk

YOUR TIME TO PRAY

Lord, I am made in Your image.
Because You walked, I learned to walk as a child.
Now I have the freedom to walk when I want to go.
But because You are my Creator, I want to walk where You walk.
And because You are my Savior, I want to walk as You direct me.
Then finally, because You live within my heart,
I want to walk where You empower me.
Amen.

9

I REST

> *On the seventh day God had finished his work of creation, so he rested from all his work.* —Genesis 2:2 NLT

In six days, I created everything—nothing existed before I began My creation activities. There was no sun, moon, or planets; including dirt and all the things that grow in dirt. There was no air. There was no time or space, there wasn't even darkness or light. For I created everything (Gen. 1:3; Isa. 45:7). There was nothing!

On the seventh day I *rested*. When you read the story, do you think I got tired? Was I creating a world more than any human can imagine? Did creation make Me weary or worn out so I needed rest? No! Did I need to replenish Myself and get a second wind as some humans need to be revitalized. Again, no!

The Hebrew word is not rest, but it is *cease*. I stopped doing the work of creation. Why? Because I was finished with the task. My planning was complete, so I didn't leave anything out. My creation was finished; I had done all I planned to do, or all I wanted to do. I ceased everything I planned to create. I finished the task of creation. I the Creator was not fatigued; I completed all I planned to create, and "it was so" (Gen. 1:9).

I used My words or voice to create all things out of nothing. That is because My words are power because they communicate My life,

My energy. Four times I described My creation. "It was good" (Gen. 1:10,12,18,21). One of My attributes is goodness—"I am good." Goodness is the highest degree of perfection. I told Moses on Mount Sinai, "And the Lord passed before him and proclaimed, 'The Lord, the Lord God, merciful and gracious, longsuffering, and abounding in goodness and truth'" (Exod. 34:6). Did you see I called Myself "good?" Some call goodness the ultimate quality of persons, whether Me (God) or you (human). But the quality read in another place said, "No one is good but One, that is, God" (Mark 10:18). *Pray: Lord, I worship Your goodness.*

The bottom line, the goodness of creation comes out of My goodness. Then look again at the creation passage. Genesis 1:31 says, "Then God saw everything that He had made, and indeed it was very good." (Gen. 1:31). That was a summary statement that My whole creation was very good.

But I didn't get tired of creating it, I didn't get tired of doing it, and I wasn't tired of anything. I rested or finished as an example to you. Just as I dedicated one day, you should do the same. Dedicate one day out of each seven days to worship, reflect, to charge yourself from weekday work to ministry work and worship. Give one day a week to Me. Follow My example and do what I did. *Pray: Lord, because You rested, I will rest.*

If I don't need to rest, but I creased My activity, you can do the same. If I don't need to prove anything about My work, but I rested, you can do the same, and make a statement to family, friends, and all others.

I am your example to cease your activity in a timely manner, in a respectful manner, and in an obedient manner.

YOUR TIME TO PRAY

Lord, You ceased Your creation on the seventh day.
It is called a day of rest.
I will follow Your example and rest once a week.
But You gave me new transforming life.
On the first day of the week.
I will honor You on Sunday with ceasing my week work.
I will worship You, serve You,
And give my life and time to You on Sunday.
Amen.

10

I THINK

> *"My thoughts are nothing like your thoughts," says the LORD. "And my ways are far beyond anything you could imagine. For just as the heavens are higher than the earth, so my ways are higher than your ways and my thoughts higher than your thoughts"* —Isaiah 55:8-9 NLT

I have thoughts, or I think; but My intellectual processes are different from yours. For you to think or have thoughts, you exercise mental activity, to bring thoughts to your awareness. There are times when you don't think, including sleeping, and there are times when you relax and drive all thoughts from your mind. But I know all thoughts of all people, at all times, and I know all things at all times. So, I know all things equally well. I don't have to think to learn something new, and I don't have to think to create a plan or answer to a problem. I know it automatically.

For some humans, when they have thoughts or they are thinking, they are comparing the past with the present. Sometimes, they are comparing the present to the future when they make plans. Future thinking and past thinking are human intellectual processes and you do one or the other. But I know the past at the same time I know the future. My Son Jesus expressed it correctly, "I am Alpha and Omega, the beginning and the end (Rev. 1:8). All of Us—the Trinity—are eternal, from eternity past to eternity future. We created time when We created the earth and the universe, and We set actions and objects into motion. Doing this, We began time. You live in both space and time. But I am above space and time. I live in the now. Past, present, and future are all an extension of My attributes. So, I don't think or have thoughts like humans. I just think everything, and I know everything.

When today's verse says, "My thoughts are not your thoughts." It explains that My thoughts are not just bigger, and faster in quality and quantity than your thoughts. No! I think using different content in My thoughts than you. I think with different mechanical processes than you. When the Scripture explains, "I call those things that are not, as though they were" (Rom. 4:17 ELT), it means I think completely different from how humans think. *Pray: Lord, thank You for writing Your thoughts in Scripture to let me know what You are thinking.*

Part of thinking has to do with expectation. You expect some things in your mind, other things you expect in your emotions. Then you will expect, or desire certain things and your mind is in sync with what you have previously decided. You expect something to happen, but it doesn't happen. Other things occur according to your expectation.

But omniscience means I know all things at all times. I know all the consequences or results of actions you plan and the consequence if they didn't happen. Now multiply all the multitude of changing consequence, with all the other multitude of changing consequence of all the decisions of all other people. A human doesn't have any idea of what they don't know. There are more than 7 billion people on the earth, plus billions from previous ages. When all the decisions of all people are added to all their differing consequences to all their possible actions, it is impossible for humans to know how many consequences there are, plus know the actions or results of them all. But I know it all and what might have happened in all situations. I call those things that are not, as though they were (Rom. 4:15). *Pray: Lord, I worship Your omniscience.*

Remember, I said in Psalm, "I, your Lord, have searched you and I know you thoroughly" (Ps. 139:1 BBJ). When I know all, there is nothing about you I don't know.

Also, "I know your thought when I am far away" (Ps. 139:2 ELT). The phrase here, "when I'm far away' refers to My localized presence, which is a reference to Me in heaven, far away from earth. But also, I am omnipresent, meaning, everywhere present at the same time. I am in you and every person on earth. I know your thoughts, their thoughts, and I know all things.

Again, "I know what you are going to say, even before you say it" (Ps. 139:4 ELT). Why is that, because I exist in the past, present, and future. I know what you will do, say, and think before any of it happens in your life.

YOUR TIME TO PRAY

Lord, one of Your greatest gifts to me,
Is my mind and the ability to think.
Because You have the ability to think,
I have the ability to think, and vision to meditate on the future.
Because I am made in Your image and likeness,
I will think my thoughts about You and worship You.
I will use my thoughts to think of ways to serve You.
I will not use my thoughts to think evil urges,
Nor will I use my mind to plan evil deeds.
Empower my mind to think great things to do for You.
Come live in my mind and let me think of You.
Amen.

11

I SEE

"I saw the God who always sees me." —Genesis 16:13 BBJ
I saw you being conceived in the protection of the womb.
—Psalm 139:15 BBJ

I am God, El Roi, the God who sees you. This name was used of Me when I revealed Myself to Hagar, Abraham's servant girl. Hagar was brought into the story because Abraham's wife, Sarah, was too old to have children. I had promised Abraham that he would have a son, but I had not yet told him how it would happen (Gen. 13:14-16). Both Abraham and Sarah thought something ought to be done.

Because Abraham was getting older, *"Sarai said to Abram, 'The Lord has prevented me from having children. Go and sleep with my servant. Perhaps I can have children through her.' And Abram agreed with Sarai's proposal. So, Sarai, Abram's wife, took Hagar the Egyptian servant and gave her to Abram as a wife"* (Gen. 16:2-3 NLT). *"...when Hagar knew she was pregnant, she began to treat her mistress, Sarai, with contempt"* (Gen. 16:4 NLT).

A great controversy erupted and Hagar ran away from the camp of Abraham. She was facing death by starvation and water depravation in the desert. The Angel of the Lord intervened to save her life and sent

Hagar back to Abraham. She called My name, El-Roi, the God who sees me.

Yes, I am El Roi, the God who saw Hagar—and I see you and everyone else. Because I am omnipresent, I am equally present everywhere at the same time. But more than everywhere at the same time, I have seen and am seeing everything in the past, including your past acts and thoughts. But I also am present everywhere equally at all places with all people now and in the future. I am El Roi, the God who sees.

But also remember, I am also the omniscient God, I know everything that is happening everywhere, at the same time, both now and in the past, and I will know in the future.

The Bible describes My eyes, this is an anthropomorphism, a human ability or attribute projected unto Me. *"The eyes of the Lord move to and fro throughout the earth..."* (2 Chron. 16:9 NASB), and *"There is no creature hidden from His sight, but all things are open and laid bare to the eyes of Him..."* (Heb. 4:13 NASB).

YOUR TIME TO PRAY

Lord, You see all things, You see my every mistake and sin,
Forgive me and cleanse me with the blood of Christ (1 John 1:7-9).
Then help me see the world through Your eyes,
And help me serve You as You want me to serve.
Help me to see You clearly as I read Your Word,
And help me understand Your will for me as I pray.
And reveal Yourself to me as I worship You.
Amen.

12

I CRY

> *Jesus wept.* —John 11:35
>
> *Jesus came close to Jerusalem and saw the city ahead, and he began to weep.* —Luke 19:41 ELT

On the east side of Jordan, known for its rugged terrain, My disciples huddled around the fire to keep warm. It was the winter of AD 29, and all they could think of was staying warm by the fire.

"Look...someone's coming." At that announcement everyone looked at the servant approaching the camp. "That's the servant of Mary and Martha...and he looks worried." The servant did not greet anyone but came straight to Me with a message.

"Lazarus is about to die; Mary and Martha want you to come immediately." The disciples looked from one worried face to another. They all realized the Jews tried to kill Me when I was recently in Jerusalem. Without saying anything, their body language indicated they didn't want to return to Jerusalem, and they didn't want Me to go there either.

I waited two days. Why? I knew what the disciples didn't know. Lazarus was dying at that very moment. Before the day would be over, Lazarus would be dead. I didn't choose to heal Lazarus at a distance, nor did I choose to leave immediately to go to the metro Jerusalem area where Lazarus lived.

Several things went through My mind while I waited. The disciples are worried about dying, but I am life. The sisters are complaining because I didn't come when they beckoned me, but I control the day a person dies.

Two days later I said, "Let's go." The disciples still didn't want to go near Jerusalem. Some were afraid that I might die; others feared for their own lives. I was sad that My followers didn't realize who I was, nor did they believe I could protect Myself. If I could heal a leper, still a storm, feed 5,000, and do many other miracles, why couldn't they believe My ability to make good choices?

It took two days to get to the outskirts of Bethany. Martha met Me with a veiled criticism. "If You had been here," she told Me, "my brother Lazarus would not have died." Martha believed I could prevent death, but she didn't believe I could raise Lazarus from the dead.

Word of My arrival reached the house where solemn Mary was mourning. She came immediately to the cemetery and said to Me the same thing as her sister, "If You had been here, my brother would not have died." It sounds like they complained to each other. Since you don't know Mary's heart, you don't know if she was trying to give Me a guilt trip or if this was outright criticism.

"He's been dead four days," the disciples may have said to each other. "What can Jesus do?"

When I got to the grave, I saw Mary weeping, and the Jews who came with her weeping. What would you expect to happen next? Here I am, the Son of God, standing in the presence of a dead corpse. Two sisters weeping. The crowd weeping. The disciples who might not have believed I could resurrect the corpse. All rejected Me in one way or another; they wouldn't recognize or believe Me.

And what did I do? I cried!

Here was a grown man crying. I was the Son of God, but I wept. Most men don't like to cry; it shows their tender side, or as they think, their weak side. Men want people to think they are strong and can endure any physical or emotional pain. Men want people to think they can overcome barriers or problems. So, men don't cry.

But I wept.

Why did I shed tears? As this story told in John 11:1-44 indicates, it is because I wanted people to believe in Me, but they didn't. I cried because of the people's unbelief in My power to raise the dead. I was the only one there who could do something about the crisis, but no one believed I could do what I was going to do.

What makes Me cry? Unbelief. When an individual refuses to believe in Me, I am brokenhearted.

Why am I brokenhearted?

- Because I died for their sins and they refuse to accept the benefits of My sacrifice.
- Because they will go to hell for all eternity where there is no escape, and there is no end.
- Because I have done all I can do to save them.
- Because they will simply not believe in Me.

Pray: Lord, I weep tears of love for Your sacrifice for me.

What makes you cry? Sometimes it's physical pain, like a broken bone or a headache. Sometimes it's because people have had something stolen from them, like a possession, money, or something valuable. Sometimes it's disappointment, whether you've disappointed yourself or someone has disappointed you. You cry when you hurt with physical or emotional pain.

But what hurts Me?

Unbelief hurts Me because it's the one thing I do not expect of My followers. I want you to trust in Me with all your heart (see Prov. 3:5). Call it trust, reliance, following, or surrender—when you believe in Me, you know that I exist, and you know I reward those who diligently seek Me (Heb. 11:6). *Pray: Lord, may I never doubt You so that I may I never make You weep.*

YOUR TIME TO PRAY

Lord, there have been times I've doubted You;
Forgive me for breaking Your heart.
There have been times when I've trusted myself,
More than trusting You—forgive me.
Lord, thank You for Your never-ending love for me.
May I never take Your love lightly,
May I never make You weep.
Amen.

Section B

LEARNING MY PERSON-LIKE REACTIONS: HOW I RESPOND

In the last section I described what appears to be My actions that relate to you and all other humans. This anthromorphism helps you understand the things I do on earth. This section describes how I react to humans. These are My responses to all human and natural stimuli.

13 – I Frown

14 – I Get Jealous

15 – I Quench (Satisfy)

16 – I Think About You

17 – I Am Sometimes Silent

18 – I Have Only Today

19 – I Remember No Longer

20 – I Plan

21 – I Choose My Leaders

22 – I Wait

23 – I Provide

24 – I Protect

25 – I Can Be Pleased

26 – I Anguish

27 – I Collect Tears In A Bottle

28 – I Have Unknowable Secrets

29 – I Don't Tell Everything

30 – I Get Angry

31 – I Hate Certain Things

32 – I Punish Sin

13

I FROWN

> "Return, faithless Israel," declares the LORD, "I will frown on you no longer...." —Jeremiah 3:12 NIV

Everyone please stay in the picture," a father pleaded with his parents and children. It was Thanksgiving Day, and he wanted to get a family portrait before everyone dove into the turkey dinner.

"I've got to go to the bathroom," a little fellow pleaded, so he took off up the stairs. A family portrait is not complete without all the little folks, so the camera had to wait.

Then a teen stepped into the family room to check on the football score, and Mother dashed into the kitchen to turn down the stove. "I'll be right back," she yelled.

When the little fellow returned, the father yelled to the teenage boy, "Come on, son!" Then he directed his irritated voice to the kitchen, "We can't take this picture without you, honey."

Finally, everyone was in place, but no one seemed happy about it. "Come on guys," the father directed his displeasure to all, "Smile."

The moment of truth arrived, so the father counted, "One, two, three...frown!" Everyone laughed, because it was the opposite of what they expected. They expected the father to command, "Smile." A frown is the opposite of a smile, and isn't a smile an upside-down frown?

Webster's tells you that the word "frown" comes from the Celtic word *foreigner*, which means to "snort" or "show facial displeasure."[1] A frown is when the disappointment you feel on the inside is seen in your face.

You frown, but can I frown? Can I feel displeasure? Yes, I can frown because I can feel displeasure when My children disobey Me or rebel against Me.

There's a second part of the definition of frown. It's when you wrinkle your forehead because you just can't figure things out. A wrinkled forehead is a frown. Am I ever in deep concentration? No! Since I know all things, there is never a time when I do not know what's going on or I can't figure things out. I am omniscient. I know all things perfectly at all times. So, when someone says I frown, it's not because I don't know what's happening. I know.

Finally, there's a third part of the definition of frown. It's when you raise an eyebrow because you are in deep thought, bewildered or can't remember. Can I forget? No, I know all things, all the time. If I didn't, then I would not be God, and that could never happen. So, I do not frown in deep thought searching for a thought I have forgotten. I know. I always know.

When I frown, it's because of My displeasure with your disobedience. Someone might ask how I can be displeased with you. Doesn't the Bible say, "The blood of Jesus Christ cleanses from all sin" (1 John 1:7)? Yes, I forgive all sins, and I cleanse your heavenly record, but there are earthly consequences to your actions. My children may lie, steal, or even kill. They shouldn't, but they do. Didn't David commit adultery and then lie to cover up the deed, finally arranging the death of Uriah to make the problem go away? The Bible says, "But the thing that David had done displeased the LORD" (2 Sam. 11:27). If you could have seen My face, I would have been frowning.

I forgave David's sin, but the results messed up the Kingdom. Yes, I cleansed David's record in heaven, but there was a baby in the palace who was conceived outside of marriage. There was a planned death of the husband. When David's general was included in the plot, David's circle of sin was extended even further.

I frowned because I had gone the extra mile to give David everything. I called David to be king over Israel. Then I gave him victory over Goliath and all the other heathen armies that attacked him. I allowed him to capture Jerusalem and then gave David a luxurious palace. In the face of My gifts, David sinned. Can you say God will frown greater if you sin in the face of My greater gifts to you? *Pray: Lord, may I never displease You.*

The verse at the beginning of this chapter declares, "'Return, faithless Israel,' declares the LORD, 'I will frown on you no longer'" (Jer. 3:12 NIV). Remember I delivered Israel from slavery in Egypt and brought her through the Red Sea. I miraculously provided water and manna in the wilderness, and then gave the Promised Land to Israel, a land flowing with milk and honey.

But Israel turned her back on Me, worshipping false idols even in My temple. Israel lived like the nations around her and committed adultery. No wonder I frowned on Israel.

But I promised, "I will frown on you no longer." What does Israel have to do to get into My pleasure? I say, "Return, faithless Israel." *Pray: Lord, I repent now of all my sins.*

Notice what happens when someone frowns. They usually want to scold or criticize, either with words or facial rejection. When you see a frown, it's a rebuke or blame. You are being admonished or reproached. You surely don't want My scolding or rejection. *Pray: Lord, don't reject me; I come humbly to You, asking for forgiveness by the blood of Christ.*

YOUR TIME TO PRAY

Lord, I want what is promised in the Levitical benediction:
Lord, may You bless me and protect me.
Lord, may You smile on me and be gracious to me.
Lord, may You show Your favor to me, and give me peace.
(Numbers 6:24-26 AMP)
Amen.

NOTE

1. Webster's New Collegiate Dictionary (Springfield, MA: Merriam-Webster Inc., 1976), s.v. "frown."

14

I GET JEALOUS

> *God is jealous...and is furious. The LORD will take vengeance on His adversaries....* —Nahum 1:2

When Elmer Towns was a freshman at Columbia Bible College, he began to fall in love with the most beautiful girl on campus, Ruth Forbes. But their first date was actually a planning session for them to date other people. On their first date, they had planned to set up Elmer's friend Dwayne Black to date Ruth. Ruth thought Dwayne was handsome and successful because he was president of their freshman class. On that date, Ruth planned to set up Mary Faith Philips to date Elmer because he thought Mary Faith was the smartest girl in their class.

After their date together, their plan worked. Elmer dated Mary Faith and Ruth dated Dwayne.

Then Ruth and Elmer had a second date to talk about their date the previous week. Then they had another date to talk about it again. They became good friends and just assumed they would go out with each other every succeeding weekend.

When Elmer found himself having some deep feelings for Ruth, a fly spoiled the ointment. Elmer's best friend Art Winn asked Ruth for a date on the same night he expected to go out with her.

Then for the first memorable time, the green-eyed monster of jealousy hit Elmer. He became furiously angry at Art—his best friend—even though they had never had a disagreement for six years. Elmer was so angry at him, he never wanted to see Art again.

Only in jealousy did Elmer realize his deep feelings for Ruth. Then Elmer told her, "I think I'm falling in love with you." Ruth told him she had thought about going out with Art but did not go through with it. Art had instigated Elmer's jealousy, not Ruth.

Jealousy is a real emotion, whether you've felt it or not. Its potential is always present. The green-eyed monster will arise whenever something comes between you and the thing you love.

When giving the Ten Commandments, I explained to My people that I could be jealous. I gave My people the first commandment: "Thou shall have no other gods before Me" (Exod. 20:3). Then I gave a second commandment that was an outgrowth of the first, saying, "You shall not make for yourself a carved image—any likeness of anything that is in heaven above, or that is in the earth beneath, or that is in the water under the earth; you shall not bow down to them nor serve them. For I, the LORD your God, am a jealous God..." (Exod. 20:4-5). Did you see how I described Myself?

I warned My people that they could make Me jealous if they let anything get between Me and them. *Pray: Lord, I confess that You have not always been first in my life. If I made you jealous and I did not know it, forgive me.*

There is a twofold action that produces jealousy: first when the object of your love turns away, and second, when the object of your love gives its love to something or someone else.

I have a jealous streak and it shows itself when My people I love turn their backs on Me and worship idols. Jealousy is the result of a broken relationship.

I Get Jealous

Is it possible for you to make Me jealous? Yes! You must not have a god between you and Me. But if you turn from Me to a false god, say, to the god of illicit sex, you make Me jealous. There are other gods that make Me jealous: the false god of entertainment, the demanding god of business success, and the god of egotistical accomplishments. While you think these things may be good in themselves, beware that they don't slip between you and Me. I am a jealous God. *Pray: Lord, I don't want to make You jealous.*

Remember, if you are My true follower, you have "Christ in you" (Col. 1:27). Paul gave this testimony, "For to me, to live is Christ..." (Phil. 1:21). I must be first in everything—first in love, first in obedience, and first in affection.

Jealousy is the back side of love. You don't get jealous over people you don't love. You're probably not even jealous when casual friends allow other things to become more important than you. You've done the same thing to some of your casual friends. While your friends seem important in your life, your children are much more important. Will your friends get jealous over your priority to your children? Probably not. The same is true with your job; you must support yourself and your family. Your casual friends don't get jealous over that.

The deepest jealousy is felt when the one you love the most turns his or her back on you to love another. I love everyone in the world, but I have a greater love for My followers who have taken up their cross to follow Me. Since I am perfect, I am perfect love. Also, since I am eternal, I have eternal love. Everything that is superior can be said about My love. So when you turn your back on perfect love, My perfect jealousy sets in. *Pray: Lord, forgive me for the times I've neglected You.*

I expect you to love Me with all your heart, soul, strength, and mind (see Matt. 22:37). Is it possible that even little things that get between you and Me makes Me jealous? Yes. Jealousy is always a possibility, and you must always strive with all your strength to put Me first in your heart. Pray: *Lord, I love You with all my heart.*

YOUR TIME TO PRAY

Lord, I know jealousy exists because I've felt my human jealousy;
So I realize that it's only natural for You to be jealous
When I put something or someone before You.
Forgive me for being callous toward You;
Forgive me for giving You second place in my life.
Lord, I realize I've spurned Your unfailing love;
Forgive me for my spiritual stupidity.
I recommit My love to You with all my heart,
And I place You at the center of my life.
Amen.

15

I QUENCH (SATISFY)

> ...*If anyone thirsts, let him come drink of Me. When someone believes in Me, I satisfy their thirst for the ultimate satisfaction in life, it is My living water that flows into your inner being.* —John 7:37-38 ELT

A woman stood as the marriage vows were repeated. This was the happiest day of her life. She was getting the thing she wanted most in life—marriage. She dreamed of this day, planned for this day, and carefully prepared for this day—a special dress, beautiful flowers, and friends and family in attendance.

What about the husband? He was nothing to brag about, just an average businessman's apprentice who promised to work hard for her and provide her a home.

After the marriage, they lived in a small room in the back of his parents' home. The big house would be theirs when the parents died, but the parents were middle-aged and in good health. They wouldn't die anytime soon. After six months, her dreams became blurry. Marriage to the young apprentice didn't make her happy, and she was getting cabin fever.

A wealthy businessman had repeatedly hired her husband to build something in his large villa. She began to dream of that home as the businessman kept adding new luxuries. The rich man had everything the young apprentice could not give his wife. The rich man had "eyes" for the apprentice's wife and was flirting with her when her husband was busy at his craft.

The businessman was sloppy, boorish, and short-tempered with people. The young girl was blinded to his unkempt body and irritable disposition. She dreamed of the villa and believed it would make her happy.

Less than a year after her first marriage, she was divorced and remarried as a trophy wife for the businessman. His villa was the mansion of her dreams.

The young wife was happy with her house for only a couple of years until it dawned upon her that bricks and mortar can't make one happy.

The young wife lost her enthusiasm for the villa and began taking long walks in the surrounding hills. She fell in love with the trees, brooks, and nature. She now looked at the world through different eyes. God's creation enchanted her, and she spent more time outdoors. She had a small garden planted near the house with a pond, trees, flowers, and some large rocks that were hauled in to make it feel like a natural pasture. But the garden didn't satisfy, so the walks in the hills became longer.

On one of her walks, she met a shepherd, and they talked of nature and God's handiwork. She began to dream of sharing her life with a soulmate. She no longer cared about a villa. She dreamed of long conversations and evenings watching the sun go down with a shepherd-lover. Her dreams of a rich villa died, and another divorce soon followed.

However, after her hasty marriage to the shepherd, she quickly found the ground too hard for sleep, and the bugs too bothersome. Sheep were dirty, and the food was not as appetizing as in the days when she thought she was in love with the shepherd.

She got tired of his dirty clothes and smelly feet. She moved into a room in town where he came to visit her every few days. Because of her fussing at him, his trips to town became less frequent.

I Quench (Satisfy)

The lonesome woman found herself spending time in the sidewalk café. She talked to all the men and fanaticized which one would make a good husband. She thought her good looks and winsome personality could catch any man she targeted.

Quickly there were two more marriages, one to the owner of the restaurant where strong drink could be purchased. She soon left him because all he wanted was someone to wait on his customers. The other was to a crotchety old man who promised her all his money if she would comfort him in his old age. She quickly tired of applying ointments, helping him walk and spoon-feeding an old man who couldn't swallow.

When she divorced the fifth husband, there was no money to pay the bills. She needed to eat, a place to sleep and to take a bath. She moved in with the town drunk. They both drank themselves to sleep at night. Now she was too drunk to dream. All of her youthful dreams faded with the realities of a harsh world.

This unnamed woman left her town of Sychar in the middle of the day to go to Jacob's Well because it was her task to fetch water for the house. Most women in Sychar went for water early in the morning and again at evening—when it was cool—where they enjoyed the company of other women and got caught up on gossip. But the town women ostracized this lonely woman because of her lifestyle, so she came by herself during the middle of the day. She had been married five times and was now living with a man though not married to him. Arriving at the well, she was startled by a Jewish man sitting on a bench. It was Me. I asked her a very simple question, "Please give Me something to drink."

April was usually hot, the temperature reaching 100 degrees during the last days of April. Because I had already walked a long distance and was hot and thirsty, I asked for a drink of water.

The woman was surprised because Jews usually didn't have anything to do with Samaritans, especially a Samaritan woman. She responded, "Why are You asking me for a drink?"

I didn't directly answer her question, but I captured her attention by saying, "But if you knew who I am, and My gift from God the Father, you would ask Me for water, and I would give you living water."

"But You don't have a rope or bucket," the woman responded. She went on to add, "The well is very deep, and there is no way for You to draw water for me."

At first the woman was concerned with the natural obstacles of getting water out of the deep well, until she realized I had promised her "living water."

"You will become thirsty after drinking water from this well," I explained to the woman, "but the water I will give to you will quench your thirst. You won't have to draw water again because My water will be an artesian well of water that will spring up within you, giving you eternal life."

"Please..." the woman begged, "give me living water so that I will never be thirsty again. I won't have to come to this well and fetch water again."

I knew the woman's heart because I Jesus was her Lord and God. I knew that her sin would have to be revealed before she would seek salvation. So, I told her, "Go call your husband."

"I don't have a husband," the woman answered Me.

"You're right..." I answered. "You don't have a husband now, but you have had five husbands and now you're not married to the man you're living with."

The woman came to the well to get natural water, but I told her I could give her "living water" to quench her thirst for worldly satisfaction. She might have thought I was offering some magical water so that she'd never have to come to the well again. In her search for satisfaction, the woman had not found it in marriage. She had searched for the perfect mate and had not found him. I said that she could find ultimate

I Quench (Satisfy)

satisfaction in worshipping God the Father (see the full story in John 4:1-42).

Just as water quenches your bodily thirst, so too fellowship with your heavenly Father quenches the yearnings of the soul. I told the woman, "The Father in heaven seeks worship from you. The Father wants you to worship Him in Spirit and truth." *Pray: Lord, I am thirsty...I need to drink from Your well.*

At another time I said, "If anyone thirsts, let him come to Me and drink. He who believes in Me, as the Scripture has said, out of his heart will flow rivers of living water" (John 7:37-38).

How can you find satisfaction? First, I tell you to come to Me. Are you thirsty? Come to Me through prayer, simply by bowing your head and talking to Me. Come to Me by listening to My Word. You do that by reading what I share with you in the Bible. Come to Me by confessing your sins so I can restore your fellowship with My heavenly Father and then you can enter My presence. If you are far way, why don't you take a first step now. *Pray: Lord, here I come. I am thirsty. I want to drink from Your well.*

You see the cup of water and you know you are thirsty. Reach out for it with your heart and lift the cup to your lips. Tilt it so that the water flows down into your soul. Taste and enjoy. *Pray: Lord, Your water is good.*

YOUR TIME TO PRAY

Lord, I've spent time and energy seeking the wrong way
To satisfy my thirst in this world.
I've learned that things and people can't satisfy me,
When I try to quench my thirst apart from You.
Lord, I realize my foolish pursuits didn't satisfy;
I repent of the silly things I did to find happiness.
I come to You now at this present time
To find happiness of soul in You.
Lord, I love You; thank You for loving me.
I come to drink and be satisfied with the water You give.
Amen.

16

I THINK ABOUT YOU

> *For I know the thoughts that I think toward you, says Me your LORD, thoughts of peace and not of evil, to give you a future and a hope.* —Jeremiah 29:11 ELT

It was nine o'clock at night on a cool June night at Camp Ben Lippen, high in the Smoky Mountains of North Carolina. Elmer Towns had just finished his freshman year at Columbia Bible College and was working to prepare the dining hall for campers the next week.

That night he was washing the winter dust from the dining room floor with a bucket, mop and a hose of running water. He was barefooted, wearing only a pair of rolled up blue jeans.

Elmer was a little disgruntled because the other two guys working with him had gone to bed, claiming to be tired. Elmer always liked to complete a job before quitting, so he told them, "You go ahead to the cabin, I will finish."

Mopping his way across the dining room, Elmer came face to face with a tattered blue sign with silver letters. A rusty nail held the sign against a 4 x 4 inch pole.

God Has A Plan For Your Life

"Ha," Elmer laughed, and then thought, "Is it God's plan for me to mop the floor while my buddies go to sleep?"

Elmer stood there staring at the sign, thinking about the words. Then he asked himself, "Does God have a plan for my life that includes working while my buddies sleep?"

"Yes," he concluded.

Elmer realized he had to live for Me not only in the big things, but also in the little things, like mopping a floor. He was not responsible for what his buddies did—he was responsible to Me for everything he did.

So, Elmer went back to mopping the floor with new enthusiasm, thinking, "I have to please God in everything, even in mopping the floor."

Do you realize that I your God think about your constantly? I say in Scripture, "For I know the thoughts that I think toward you" (Jer. 29:11).

Some people never realize I think. Just as you have the power to think, feel, and make choices, I—in whose image you were created— have intellect, emotion, and will. When I bent over the lifeless clay man, the one later called Adam, I breathed My breath into Adam, "and man became a living soul" (Gen. 2:7). *Pray: Lord, I am awed at the sight of the Divine breathing life into a lifeless clay man. Thank You for giving me life—Your life.*

I do not have a physical body, but I have the power of mind—I think; I have the power of emotions—I love; I have the power of will—I choose.

Because I have a mind, I remember. Because I see your sins. *Pray:* "Do not remember the sins of my youth" (Ps. 25:7).

You must constantly pray, "Remember me, O LORD" (Ps. 106:4). Isn't that what the thief on the cross asked of Me, "Remember me when You come into Your kingdom?"

When you remember, you give effort to recall what you previously experienced. Like the student studying for an exam, you memorize so you can recall facts for a test. But I do not have to give effort to recall. If I did, that would say I at one time did not know everything. That cannot happen. Why? Because I know all things without effort at all times.

What else do I do with My mind? I reason. Did not I say, "Come now, and let us reason together...though your sins are like scarlet, they shall be as white as snow; thought they are red like crimson, they shall be as wool" (Isa. 1:18). When I invite you to reason with Me, I want you to understand that I know all about your sin. When you confess your sins and correct your evil ways by repenting, I know. When you ask for forgiveness, I cleanse you as white as snow. *Pray: Lord, I accept Your invitation. Make my heart white as snow. I confess I am a sinner...I have sinned.*

Since I have made you in My image (see Gen. 1:26-27), your ability to think, feel, and choose comes from Me. When you look into the mirror each morning to comb your hair, you see an image of yourself. What you see is a reflection of who you are; but it is not you, you see your image. When I look into your face, I see My image. In one sense, I see Myself when I look at you. You are like Me, but you are not Deity.

I have given you many powers of the mind. You think because I think, and your thoughts guide your life. You remember because I know everything actual and potential. So you bring past experiences into your mind to help you guide today's activities. You have the power of choice because I exercise My will and as you understand your choices, you better control your life.

I think about you constantly. You are never out of My mind. Though there are billions of people in the world, I can think about each one at the same time. I am unlimited. No one is ever out of My thoughts. *Pray: God, You overwhelm me. You are much bigger than any conception I have of You. Help me think properly about all things; help me think accurately of You.*

YOUR TIME TO PRAY

Lord, You thought up a good plan for my life;
Thank You for thinking good things of me.
I want to know Your plan for my life,
I want the good things You have been thinking.
Lord, teach me to think my thoughts after You,
I yield my thoughts to Your superior plan;
I will to do Your will.
Amen.

17

I AM SOMETIMES SILENT

> *You ask, "Why do I stand afar off?" Also you ask, "Why are You silent in times of my trouble?"* —Psalm 10:1 ELT
>
> *You ask, "How long will You forget me, O LORD?" And, "How long will You hide Your face from me?"*
> —Psalm 13:1 ELT

Jerry Falwell, pastor of Thomas Road Baptist Church for more than 50 years, died suddenly at 10:31 a.m. on May 15, 2007. As the ambulance rushed to his office, the airwaves at Liberty University were overloaded with news of the emergency. It seemed every phone in the university rang at the same time. Everyone quickly heard the news, and everyone's grief was different. Some reacted with explosive weeping; others were too stunned to respond.

Then the announcement went out—students and employees were told to gather in the church sanctuary at 1:30 p.m. That was a chapel service no one would miss. No one would skip this meeting. Jerry was dead, and everyone had questions.

Silently, everyone entered the huge 6,000-seat sanctuary. No one talked; no one whispered. The organ was not playing. Those with red eyes caught a glimpse of other eyes still crying. Some cried inwardly. The only sound was rustling of clothes, feet shuffling on the carpet, and the dull groan of theater seats being occupied. Finally, everyone was seated.

Silence.

The only thing heard was the sound of silence. When there is no noise, your ears are alert to hearing anything, but there was nothing to hear. Only an occasional cough or sniffle. Then even those coughing tried to muffle their sound.

When silence surrounds you, several different emotions capture your thinking. Usually you focus on why you are being quiet. Everyone was thinking about Jerry. Why would I his God and daily Guide take him? What is going to happen now? Why did I the God of the living let him die?

Then people's thoughts turned inward. What will I do? Many were thinking, "How will this affect me...my future?"

There was a silence in the room that day even though there were several thousand people present. It was not eerie or scary. It was not even threatening. It was simply reverent silence. Everyone waited in My presence, the God of Jerry Falwell, wondering in unison: *God, why did You take Jerry Falwell?*

All sensed their corporate grief so the meeting did not begin immediately. Silence had its healing ministry.

Why is it that you are asked to be silent in My presence? The Bible says, "The LORD is in His holy temple. Let all the earth keep silence before Him" (Hab. 2:20). Sometimes I do not want you to talk to Me or even praise Me. Sometimes I want you to be quiet and think about Me.

You may feel nothing is happening when people are silent, but when the mouth is quiet, the heart, soul, and mind are actively engaged.

In silence, people repent of their sins.

In silence, people mediate on the Scriptures and grow spiritually.

I Am Sometimes Silent

In silence, people stand in awe of Me.

In silence, people wait for Me to speak to them.

Sometimes, I reveal Myself in loud thunder and with crashing lightning. In those moments, My loud, compelling voice can be heard over the noise of daily life. But at other times, I speak in a still, quiet voice, and it is only in silence that you can hear My heart and My message. Did not I say, "Be still and know that I am God" (Ps. 46:10)? *Pray: Lord, I am not talking. I am quiet. Speak to me.*

There are times when you feel My presence in quietness, but you miss Me in the thunderous noise surrounding you. Remember the story of My Son Jesus sending His disciples in a boat into a storm. Because He knows everything—better than a weathercaster does—Jesus knew a killer storm was waiting to attack them. When the storm struck, the disciples screamed in panic. You can almost hear them yelling, their screams louder than the sound of the storm. Can you imagine the scared prayers coming from that little boat?

Then Jesus came walking to them on the water. In the midst of noise, the wind, and the crashing waves, Jesus came to them and spoke, "Peace, be still" (Mark 4:39). Can you imagine the emotional shock of the disciples when the stormy lake instantly quieted into the night? Suddenly the clouds were gone, the moon and stars twinkled, and there was nary a breeze blowing. On a calm lake, the disciples worshipped their Lord who was Jesus. *Pray: Lord, calm my inner storms and give peace to my heart.*

When Jerry Falwell died, everyone focused on his or her hurt and loss. No one realized I was about to do supernatural things for the church and the university. Jonathan, Jerry's youngest son, would immediately step in to carry Thomas Road Baptist Church to even greater heights. Over the next five months, more than 1,000 people came to receive Christ, and more than 1,200 would join the church.

Then there was Jerry Jr., the oldest son who became president and chancellor of Liberty University. The following semester after Jerry Sr.

died, attendance reached the first goal that Jerry Sr. had set more than thirty years earlier—enrolling 25,000 students at the university. Three months after Jerry Sr. died, more than 28,000 students enrolled on campus and in the distance-learning program under Jerry Jr.'s new leadership.

Do not fear silence. It is in silence that you can hear Me, your Lord God speak to you. Seek silence, for in the quiet place, you will find Me.

YOUR TIME TO PRAY

Lord, thank You for speaking clearly in the Scriptures;
Thank You for silence when I listen to hear and understand Your will.
Lord, I wait silently and reverently in Your presence;
Speak for I am listening for Your voice.
Lord, I will do what You tell me to do.
I want to please You with my life.
Amen.

18

I HAVE ONLY TODAY

> *And of the children of Issachar, which were men that had understanding of the times, to know what Israel ought to do....* —1 Chronicles 12:32 KJV
>
> *"I am the Alpha and the Omega, the Beginning and the End,"* says the Lord, *"who is and who was and who is to come, the Almighty."* —Revelation 1:8

Two pilots were flying a large airliner cross-country. The copilot asked the senior pilot why he always flew nearly fifty miles out of the way over a little town in Kansas on their cross-country flights. The older replied, "I was raised in that little town, and I always look for the only river in the area on the south of the city."

"Why is that?" the copilot asked, knowing there was a story there.

"I used to fish on the bank of that river and lay in the grass to dream of what I'd do when I grew up. I'd always dream of flying a plane. I figured when I got to be a pilot, I'd be the happiest in life. I never really thought I'd ever get out of that little town."

Within a few minutes the plane approached the little town, and the pilot dipped his wings in salute to the river he had just described.

"Why'd you do that?" the copilot absent-mindedly asked.

The pilot wistfully answered, "I thought I'd be ultimately happy when I got out of that town and got to be a pilot, but I'm not." The senior pilot poured out his problems with his kids, overspent credit cards, drinking addiction, and suspected infidelity of his wife. Then he looked back once more and said, "I didn't realize how happy I was lying in the grass by that river until I left it."

Do you realize that today is the most important day in your life? Today is the tomorrow you dreamed of yesterday. If you're not happy *now*, you won't be happy tomorrow because if you don't learn to live *now* and get the most out of *now*, you will never enjoy tomorrow. *Pray: Lord, I want to be happy now!*

When you reflect on My heart, you'll realize how urgent *today* is. I have given you the gift of time. I didn't give you the eighteenth century; I gave you *now*, so you must use what I have given you today. There's a reason why you are the child of your parents and not the reverse. Find out what I want you to do today and do it now. Do not put it off until tomorrow, which may never come. *Pray: Lord, help me find happiness in today.*

For instance, you can learn how to live *now* when you know the benefits of yesterday. Yesterday had power and is the foundation of today. It was a school to prepare you to live today. If you didn't learn yesterday's lessons yesterday, then determine to learn them today. That way today will be the school that will prepare you for tomorrow. Then tomorrow will be the *TODAY* that you spent getting ready for yesterday. *Pray: Lord, let me learn from yesterday for a better today.*

Understand the power of tomorrow. Your dreams will be realized in your tomorrows, and those dreams will give energy to your life today. Dreams will drive you to work harder to accomplish them. Dreams will discipline you to sacrifice to obtain them. Dreams have the power to make you learn from yesterday so you can prepare for tomorrow. *Pray: Lord, let my dreams motivate me to prepare for tomorrow.*

Finally, learn the urgency factor of today. Why? Because while it is important to dream and plan for the future, it is also important to live in today. Live one day at a time and don't get overly anxious about what the future holds (see Matt. 6:34). When tomorrow comes, it won't be tomorrow—it will be today. You can only live one day at a time, and that day is today. *Pray: Lord, I will live now for You. Help me get everything possible out of now.*

Let's think about the sons of Issachar described in the opening verse from 1 Chronicles. They knew the times in which they lived. Notice the verse doesn't describe their past or their future, nor did it say they understood their past or their future. The fact they knew their present times meant they learned from the school of yesterday and the dreams of tomorrow motivated their today. "They knew the times." *Pray: Lord, help me see my world through Your eyes, and help me know today.*

You can't know everything. There's no PhD in history who knows all about the many yesterdays that have ever existed. Only I know all about yesterday because I was there. Learn from Me so you'll be prepared to live today.

You can't know everything about the future. You'll never live in the tomorrow of the future. You'll only live a succession of todays. But I am already living at the day of your death. I know when it'll happen, where it'll happen, and how it'll happen. Since there is no yesterday or tomorrow for Me, let Me prepare you to live today, so you'll be prepared when it comes time to die. *Pray: Lord, I commit my death to You.*

The sons of Issachar not only knew the times, they knew what Israel ought to do. That suggests two or three things they knew. They knew the Scriptures where I predicted the future of Israel and how Israel should be living for Me. They also knew Me, their God and how I related to My people. Finally, they knew what was right, and what Israel had to do to get right with Me and to live for Me. *Pray: Lord, may I know the times as did the sons of Issachar, and may I do right.*

There is coming a day when there'll be no more time. It'll be eternal day, an eternal *NOW*. In that future day, there will be no more tomorrows to motivate you to action and self-improvement. There will be no more night. Then you'll be like the sons of Issachar; you'll know the times, and you'll know what to do.

Another thing about your future day in heaven is that there'll be no yesterdays to teach you how to live. You will know all you are supposed to know, and you will do all you are supposed to do. There'll be no regrets in heaven over your failures of yesterday. There'll be "no more crying" (Rev. 21:4) and no memory to take away your joy. You shall be perfect like Me when you see My face (see 1 John 3:2; Rev. 22:4).

YOUR TIME TO PRAY

Lord, I've had a lot of failures in my yesterdays,
Forgive me for each and every one.
Lord, my tomorrows are not much better;
I've failed to accomplish much because of my past.
Lord, I didn't take care of all my todays;
Forgive me of all my failures and sins,
Those that involved my yesterdays, tomorrows, and todays.
Lord, I look forward to Your eternal day;
Maybe it will come tomorrow,
Then I'll live perfect with You.
But, if it doesn't come for a long time,
I'll live for You today.
Amen.

19

I REMEMBER NO LONGER

> *...I will forgive their iniquity, and their sin I will remember no more.* —Jeremiah 31:34

Young Johnnie got a new slingshot and tried it out in the backyard of his grandmother's farm. He shot at the barn door and missed. He shot at the gate and missed. He shot at some birds flying overhead and missed. Then, he went down by the stream, shot at a snake, and missed.

Walking back into the farmyard, he shot at Grandmother's favorite duck and hit it in the head, killing it instantly. He looked both ways and thought, "No one saw me." He quickly got a shovel out of the tool shed and buried the duck behind the barn.

That night after supper Grandmother asked Johnnie's sister, "Mary Jane, will you wash the dishes?"

"No," she said deviously, "Johnnie likes to wash dishes." Then she whispered to him, "Remember the duck."

Johnnie gladly washed dishes since he was afraid of what would happen if Grandmother found he had killed her pet duck.

The next morning after breakfast, Grandmother asked Mary Jane to sweep the hall and porch. She answered, "No ma'am, Johnnie likes to sweep." Then she whispered, "Remember the duck."

That week Johnnie swept the hall every morning, washed dishes after every meal, and did every other task his sister Mary Jane wanted him to do.

The next Saturday morning, Johnnie could not take it any longer. He told his grandmother the story of killing her favorite duck. Through his tears Johnnie sobbed, "I'm sorry."

"I know," Grandmother said, "I was washing dishes at the window when I saw you hit my duck. I saw the panic on your face, and I know you didn't mean to do it."

"Did you give him a nice burial?" Grandmother asked.

"Yes," Johnnie answered, "but why did you wait so long to forgive me?"

"I forgave you the moment I saw the anguish in your face," Grandmother replied, "but I wondered how long you'd stay in bondage to Mary Jane."

Many are in bondage to a sin they committed in the past. They go through life blaming themselves for something they did. Their conscience—their own Mary Jane—whispers, "Remember the duck."

When people are convicted by a past sin, they often spend their lives in miserable bondage. Everyone needs to remember My promise found in 1 John 1:7 ELT, "The blood of Me, Jesus Christ, God's Son, cleanses you from all sin." Just as Grandmother forgave Johnnie the moment he killed her duck, so My Father forgives you the moment you sin. That is the nature of My Father's forgiveness.

Instead of enjoying My freedom, some Christians walk around dejectedly in bondage. They are slaves to the sin they have committed.

The Bible has the promise, "I will forgive their iniquity, and their sin I will remember no more" (Jer. 31:34). Notice it does not say I forget your sin. Why? I know all things at all times. If I forget and do not know what happened that would breach My nature. If I forget that, that would not be God-like, or reject the truth of My divine nature.

"I remember no more." When I do that—you can say I choose to remember no more—I am still omniscient. I am in charge. Your sins are buried in the deepest sea (see Micah 7:19). I know they are there, but I choose not to remember.

There are two steps to forgiveness. The first is a picture of the grandmother looking out the window to see her favorite duck killed. That is a picture of Me, your heavenly Father looking out the window of heaven to see your sin. I forgive you the moment you sin because "the blood of Jesus Christ, His Son, cleanses us from all sin" (1 John 1:7 AMP).

The second step is Johnnie going to his grandmother to confess his sin because he has offended her and hurt her. Johnnie killed her favorite duck. That is a picture of you going sorrowfully to Me, your Father to confess and make things right. "If we confess our sins, He is faithful and just to forgive us our sins and cleanse us from all unrighteousness" (1 John 1:9).

I your Father forgave you before you confess, but you must come to Me and tell Me you are sorry. You do not confess for My sake; you must confess for your sake. *Pray: Lord, I honestly confess I have sinned. Forgive me—I need cleansing.*

There is a difference between your relationship and your fellowship with Me, your heavenly Father. I instantly forgive you when you sin because of your relationship to Me. I am your heavenly Father, and you are My child. That relationship cannot be broken.

But your fellowship with Me is another matter. Fellowship describes your joyful approach to Me. Nothing can affect your eternal relationship with Me, your heavenly Father, but your sin can convict you and steal your happiness. You must come to Me when your fellowship is broken and tell Me you are sorry and ask Me to restore your fellowship.

YOUR TIME TO PRAY

Heavenly Father, thank You for the blood of Christ, my Savior
That cleanses me of all sin;
I accept Your grace and walk in Your mercy;
Thank You for forgiving me before I ask.
But Father, when I slip and fall into sin;
I am sorry for my sin, that I didn't mean to do;
Forgive me and restore my fellowship with You.
Amen.

20

I PLAN

> *"For I know the plans I have for you," says the Lord. "They are plans for good and not for disaster, to give you a future and a hope."* —Jeremiah 29:11 NLT
>
> *I will show you the path of life; in My presence is fullness of joy; at My right hand are pleasures forevermore.*
> —Psalm 16:11 ELT

Did you know I have a plan for My people? That means I have a wonderful plan for your life. Have you found it? Are you following it? Some people call "My plan" by My volitional choice then call it *the will of God*.

People spend lots of time planning. They plan for vacations and for special nights out with their spouse. They make plans for the direction of their career and the growth of a family business. They like to make a plan for their day, their year, even their lifetime. What are you plans?

I your Lord and God have plans for you, because I want to do good things for you. However, I didn't complete all the good things I had planned for Adam and Eve in the Garden of Eden because of their sin and rebellion to Me. The same with every other person being born on earth, I cannot do all the good things I planned for them because people choose to go their own way or do things apart from Me, or they rebel and sin against My standards (Ten Commandments), or My Word.

But before we look at the consequences, let's examine the nature and definition of *plan*. To plan is to decide or arrange things in advance of what will happen, or what will be built or put together. A plan is a detailed proposal for doing something in the future or getting something you presently do not have. Sometimes a plan can be described as a blueprint, a prescription, a prototype of what an object will be and do in the future; it could be a proposal or orthographic projection of future object or foundation of the object.

When you use the word *plan*, you usually begin with a vision of what you see in your mind, or projection of how something will work, or give service to you. A plan is developed to guarantee success or meaningful function in the future, such as business plans, or marketing plans, or a set of principles and/or rules to guide to future success.

When you are in the process of planning, you are doing several functions. You are devising or plotting, or drafting, or sketching, or developing aims or purposes, or you are dividing your intentions. Basically, you are meditating, contemplating, developing a master plan or a game plan or road map.

However, I the Lord God of the ages created time: "In the beginning I created the heavens and the earth" (Gen. 1:1 ELT). What is time? Time is the distance between objects. When I created the first thing or object and it took form to begin its existence, then the distance between the first object and when I created the second object is called *time*.

There is no time with Me. I am always present in the past, present, and future. I am eternal God, so I have existed forever in the past and will exist forever in the future. Remember, I am not controlled by time, I control time and My actions are beyond the time of past, present, and future.

I know everything possible, and I know at all times, past, present, and future. So, there was never a time when I didn't know everything about everything. Therefore, it is inconceivable to humans to think of Me planning, because to make plans is to project present activities into the future. So, how could I the eternal God who knows all things make a plan?

"'For I know the thoughts that I think toward you,' says the LORD, 'thoughts of peace and not of evil, to give you a future and a hope'" (Jer. 29:11). When I told Jeremiah "I know the plans I have for you," I was using the human expression of making plans for an event or action that had not yet occurred. That is contradictory for Me, for I can never make a future plan, because I already am existing in the future, when the plan will become a reality. This is an anthromorphism—a projection onto deity a function or attribute of a human. So when I tell you I have plans for you, I want you understand My desire for you to act in faith, obedience, and fellowship with Me.

So, what does that mean? Since I tell you "I have plans for you," it is what I want you to become and do just as I expect you to make plans for your life and then do them by faith and obedience.

But I also expect you to make good plans, not evil plans, or self-centered plans that will lead you away from My will for your life. If I can make good plans for you, I expect you to make good plans for your marriage, vacation, service at your church—every aspect of your life. Follow My example so I can do good things for you, "to give you a future and a hope" (Jer. 29:11 NLT).

After Adam and Eve sinned against Me (Rom. 5:12), I developed a plan to save Adam and all humans from the torment of hell. Not only did I want Adam and all humans who live after him to be saved, I want them to live according to My will by obeying the directions of Scripture. In the Bible you find principles and promises that will do you "good" and not lead to disaster.

I want you as a human to make good plans for yourself, your family, and your church. Then live by the plans you make. When you are reflecting My plan, you are implementing My nature and life into your daily routine—for good.

So what can you learn about My plans for you?

First, I have a plan for every person to turn to Me and follow Me. "I am not willing that any should perish" (2 Peter 3:9 ELT). But there is a problem! All are sinners and sin keeps all from salvation. The Bible says, "All have sinned" (Rom. 3:23), and Psalm 51 states that all were born sinners, "in sin my mother conceived me" (Ps. 51:5).

But I planned to overcome this sin obstacle. I your heavenly Father sent My sinless Son to be born into this world and live among sinful people. It was My desire that all would be saved: "Behold! The Lamb of God who takes away the sin of the world!" (John 1:29).

When you become My follower, My disciple, I have a plan for you. Jesus said, "My Father, who has given them to Me, is greater than all: and no one is able to snatch them out of My Father's hand" (John 10:29). I plan to keep you eternally when I gave you eternal life. *Pray: Lord, I rest in Your plans for my eternal life.*

I plan good things for My followers. My Son Jesus said, "I have come that they may have life, and that they may have it more abundantly" (John 10:10). The first promise is "eternal life" in heaven. The second is an abundantly good life on earth after they are saved. *Pray: Lord, give me abundance in my life as I live for You on this earth.*

I want you to choose to follow My plans for your life. I said, "I am the Door; anyone who enters through Me will be saved [and will live forever], and will go in and out [freely] and find pasture (spiritual security) (John 10:9 AMP). I do not make you follow Me, but when you choose to follow Me, your faithfulness is rewarded. *Pray: Lord, I need Your deliverance from sin to accomplish Your good plans for my life.*

I have plans for your success. Do not humans have dreams for success? A high school girl dreams of becoming the homecoming queen, and the high school boy dreams of becoming the winning quarterback on the school's team. And doesn't every insurance sales representative want to be a member of the million-dollar round table? I plan for your success, but you must live according to the plans I have for you and your success. What are these plans? I promised, "This Book of the Law shall not depart from your mouth, but you shall read [and meditate on] it day and night... then you will make your way prosperous, and then you will be successful" (Josh. 1:8 AMP). *Pray: Lord, I will follow Your instructions so I will be successful.*

Yes, I have a wonderful plan for you and everyone else. I want everyone to experience My love and salvation, and become a dedicated disciple of My Son, Jesus Christ.

But what happens when you or anyone ignores Me and strays from My plan in the Word of God? Those who have turned their backs on Me have missed the wonderful opportunities I want to provide for them and the eternal salvation I offer them. Some of My followers are missing out on the good impact I intended for their lives.

Just imagine––what if there was no Winston Churchill to rally the Allies against Hitler? What if there was no George Washington to get America through Valley Forge and ultimately win the American Revolution. What if there was no Martin Luther or John Wesley?

Think about your life and what you could accomplish. I love you and have a special plan for your life. Do you know what it is? My plan should become clearer to you each day of your life. "But the path of the just (righteous) is like the light of dawn, that shines brighter and clearer until [it reaches its full strength and glory in] the perfect day" (Prov. 4:18 AMP). As you follow Me, your Lord, My plan for your life will become brighter and brighter.

If you are not aware that I your Lord have a plan for your life, then start a twofold process. First, the Bible says you can find My will and know it: "Understand what the will of the Lord is" (Eph. 5:17). Second, yield your life right now to Me. From now on, make sure that you do what I want you to do. *Pray: Lord, I want to follow Your plan for my life. Show it to me and I will start walking.*

I want you to plan your life in accordance with My plans. An architect draws a blueprint of what he wants to accomplish, then the workers follow the plans to construct a building in accord with the pre-drawn plans. Therefore, you must work diligently to live your life in accordance with My pre-determined plans. *Pray: Lord, I will study Your blueprint for my life. Then I will daily live what You pre-determine for me to be and do.*

Sometimes a worker runs into problems as he constructs a building. There may be unseen bedrock or an unexpected stream of underground water. When digging a foundation for a dormitory at Liberty University in 2006, such a spring was discovered and the whole dorm was moved hundreds of yards.

In your life the onset of problems or sin may mean a change of plans. A young man graduated from Liberty University and planned to go to the mission field, but his wife refused. As she was working to put her husband through seminary, she discovered a world of entertainment and fun that she enjoyed. She divorced the future missionary. The future missionary had to change his plans. What happens when sin or your disobedience or your laziness disrupts your plans? *Pray: Lord, forgive me when I have messed up. I want to get back into the center of Your plans.*

A global positioning system (GPS) gives you directions to any place in the United States. You can find your way to any church, hotel, or restaurant with the touch of a button. When you choose a destination, it guides you there on the closest route. But when you miss a turn, a voice says, "Recalculating." In your Christian life, that is probably your conscience speaking to you. Or it may be a Christian friend. Then the GPS gives you another route based on your new location.

If you miss My primary plan for your life, I can give you another plan. My plan is much like a GPS. When you take a wrong turn, I do not drop you. No, I want you to glorify Me and serve Me. I *recalculate* and give you the best plan for the rest of your life from your new location. *Pray: Lord, thank You for forgiving my past sins and failures. Thank You for every time You have "recalculated" Your plan for my life.*

YOUR TIME TO PRAY

Lord, thank You for Your good plans for me.
Forgive me when I have sinned and missed Your direction.
I will turn away from selfishness and evil,
And look only to You to guide me into Your plans.
I will follow Your plans as You show them to me.
I was lost and doing my own thing.
Thank You for saving me and giving me a new purpose.
Now help me glorify You and serve You in all I do.
Lord, I find happiness and pleasure in fulfilling Your plans.
Keep me in the center of Your will.
If I ever stray from doing Your plan,
Bring me back and recalculate my life.
Amen.

21

I CHOOSE MY LEADERS

...Before you were born I set you apart and appointed you as my prophet to the nations. —Jeremiah 1:5 NLT

for you are a people holy to the LORD your God. Out of all the peoples on the face of the earth, the Lord has chosen you to be his treasured possession. —Deuteronomy 14:2 NIV

Ye have not chosen me, but I have chosen you, and ordained you, that ye should go and bring forth fruit.... —John 15:16 KJV

But God chose the foolish things of the world to shame the wise; God chose the weak things of the world to shame the strong. God chose the lowly things of this world and the despised things—and the things that are not—to nullify the things that are, so that no one may boast before him. —1 Corinthians 1:27-29 NIV

I the Lord of the universe and God of creation, choose leaders based on a diffident standard than people choose a political leader, or those in business chose a president or executive director. The Scriptures tell stories of My effective leaders—both men and women—who were chosen to serve Me. Some were kings, judges, priests, prophets, disciples, and average church workers.

Look at My choice of David as king of Israel for forty years. Samuel, My prophet, went to David's home looking for a leader. I told him, "I have provided me a king" (1 Sam. 16:1 KJV). When Samuel arrived, the boastful father Jessie had his sons presented to Samuel: *"But the Lord said unto Samuel, Look not on his countenance, or on the height of his stature; because I have refused him:* [Jesse's first candidate], *for the Lord seeth not as man seeth; for man looketh on the outward appearance, but the Lord looketh on the heart"* (1 Sam. 16:7 KJV).

Because I know all things large and small, and both inward and outward. I know what is in a person's heart (Job 34:21; Heb. 4:13). As Samuel looked at all the fine young sons of Jesse, not one of them was qualified in God's sight. Finally Jesse had to send for his youngest son, David, who was faithfully watching sheep in the fields. No one in the crowd thought of David, but God knew his heart.

Moses was 80 years old, too elderly by today's standards, but God chose him, called him, and used Moses to first of all deliver God's people from the tyrannical slavery of Egypt, breaking the stronghold of the most power nation in the world at that time. Then in the second place, God used Moses to lead His people through the wilderness—forty years because of their disobedience—to the Promised Land.

David made several mistakes in his life, even though he began as God's champion. Yet through his adultery, murder of Uriah, political choices and family problems, God still used David. In the same way, God used Moses in spite of his arrogance to think he was to bring water out of the rock. Moses was punished to not enter the Promised Land, yet God used Moses to deliver His people, organize them into a fighting unit, build the tabernacle and instruments in the tabernacle, plus continually deal with rebellious Israel who complained until the last of that generation died in the desert. *Pray: Lord, thank You for choosing me, I will not resist Your leadership.*

How did David and Moses perform? As long as they followed Me and carried out My will, I continued to use them.

YOUR TIME TO PRAY

God, could use me to accomplish a great work for You?
Only You know the heart of those You choose leaders.
Lord, I will be ready to do anything in Your service,
So, when You chose me for leadership,
I will serve gratefully.
Amen.

22

I WAIT

> *Therefore the LORD will wait, that He may be gracious to you; and therefore...blessed are all those who wait for Him.*
> —Isaiah 30:18

Some people are impatient, whether it is waiting in a long line of shoppers or waiting when they are caught in traffic gridlock. Other people are easy going. They know there is not much they can do about long lines. So, in the car they may listen to some praise worship CDs, or if they are waiting for a delayed airplane, they listen to their iPod.

Look again at that impatient person. It is not that they get irritated with someone who wastes their time or are frustrated with a traffic jam. What irks them is the feeling that they are missing out on doing something profitable. They are good with time management. They have the day planned and their desk organized so they can get as much done as possible. They do not like to wait because they feel it is wasting time. When external forces hold them back, they get impatient because of all the things they could be doing.

Have you ever thought that I your God have to wait? Most think that I am all-powerful, and I just make everything happen. So, I do not have to wait. But the Bible teaches that I wait. Why do I wait and how do I deal with it?

I have a purpose when I am waiting. I wait for people to repent of sin and turn to Me. I do not immediately judge every sin when it is committed. I give people an opportunity to turn to Me for forgiveness. *Pray: Thank You, Lord, for Your patience with me.*

I know all things. I know those who will get saved and those who will not. Time does not constrain Me. I live in the past, present, and future. Right now, I am in the present, this day, this minute. I know those who will not believe, but I give them a complete calendar of pre-determined days to live. I wait on them.

Sometimes, even though I answer your prayers immediately, I have to wait to see the fruit of your response. When you beg Me for money for your church, I do not instantly make cash appear. Sometimes when you pray, I touch the heart of someone to give the money who answers your prayers. But then there are the logistical steps that have to take place; the person has to write a check and mail it. Sometimes the person neglects to go swiftly to the mailbox, and sometimes the mail is delayed. Even though you may think that I have said "No," in actuality you just have to be patient to allow My process to work.

The same process happens when you pray for healing. Suppose you ask Me to heal someone. The sick do not usually spring up immediately out of bed and go back to work. Health and strength return slowly. I could heal instantly by taking away a germ or infection. But doesn't it take time for inflections to be flushed out of the body's system? Maybe the sick person needs sleep and food to gain strength. I heal, and then I sit back to wait for healing to strengthen the whole body.

Jeremiah reminds you of My promise, "I bring upon them all the good that I have promised them" (Jer. 32:42). I have good plans for your life. But you might have some rebellion within and do not follow Me in every small way that you should. So, I cannot give you the good things I have promised. I have to work My good plan through detours and some side excursions. I wait to give you good things. *Pray: Thank You, Lord, for waiting with patience.*

I want to use you, but you are not always spiritual enough or prepared enough. A young preacher's first sermon may be a flop. He may preach three minutes and run out of stuff to say. He may give a gospel invitation, and nothing happens. Perhaps I could not use the young man because he wasn't ready to be used. I may have to wait until he becomes useable, more mature.

In the same way, I wait for you to become more mature in faith so that I can use you for My purpose. I am patient to unfold the plans I have for your life. *Pray: Lord, thank You for not giving up on me, thank You for Your patience.*

YOUR TIME TO PRAY

Lord, patience is one of Your attributes;
Thank You for being patient with me.
Lord, if You judged every sin immediately,
I would not last long on this earth.
Lord, I need patience to be more like you.
Teach me when to wait patiently
And when to stubbornly push ahead.
Amen.

23

I PROVIDE

> *And Abraham called the name of the place, Jehovah-Jireh, (I the LORD will provide); as it is said to this day, "In this Mount, I the LORD shall provide."*
> —Genesis 22:14 ELT

Early one morning, I called Abraham to go to a mountain that would be shown to him. He was told to offer his son Isaac as a sacrifice to Me. The language meant Isaac was to be offered physically as a burnt offering. Some Bible translators call it a "whole burnt offering" in which the sacrifice was burned up completely in gratitude or worship of Me.

This was an astonishing request. I promised Abraham a son through whom the Messiah would come who would free the world. I also promised he would make a great nation through his son Isaac. Anyone else might have doubted My request, but Abraham obeyed Me and believed that "I was able to raise [Isaac] up from the dead" (Heb. 11:19 ELT). And there is another picture to see in this story: the mountain to which I would lead Abraham is the same mountain where the fulfillment of My ultimate plan would be take place. This is the mountain where My Son would eventually be crucified and die.

When I called Abraham, the old patriarch answered, "Here I am," showing his obedience to Me (Gen. 22:1). Here is where Abraham became a man of faith. I called him My friend (see Isa. 41:8; 2 Chron. 20:7). Later in the New Testament, James writes, "And the Scripture was fulfilled which says, 'Abraham believed God, and it was accounted to him for righteousness.' And he was called the friend of God" (James 2:23).

When Abraham and Isaac got to the top of the mountain, the young Isaac asked, "Look, the fire and the wood, but where is the lamb for a burnt offering?" (Gen. 22:7).

The father answered prophetically, "My son, God will provide for Himself the lamb for a burnt offering" (Gen. 22:8). Abraham's answer provides a prediction of the substitutionary death of My Son, Jesus Christ who died for you.

When Abraham lifted his arm with knife in hand to take the life of his son, I called him by name, "Abraham!" (Gen. 22:11). With the same obedience that he began the journey, Abraham again answered, "Here I am" (Gen. 22:11).

Because of Abraham's obedience, I provided the sacrificial animal. Abraham saw a ram caught in thick vines by its horns—so it would be unblemished. Abraham offered the ram as a whole burnt offering of praise and worship to Me and named the place "Jehovah-Jireh," which means "I your God supplies."

You can learn two lessons from this event. First, on this mountain I "provided Myself" as the sacrificial lamb who died for the sins of the world. Calvary is "Jehovah-Jireh," the place I your God provided salvation for you. *Pray: Lord, thank You for providing for my salvation.*

The second lesson is that I will provide for you. But you must be careful when you ask for My provision. Do not be like the lazy ministerial student who said he was trusting Me to provide his finances when in actuality he was lazy, didn't work for money, and didn't really intercede that deeply. He had empty faith when claiming "Jehovah-Jireh."

The China Inland Mission was the first great "Faith Foreign Mission Board." Some of the greatest and godliest missionaries evangelized inland China without a guaranteed salary, trusting Me to supply all their financial needs. Over the door to their headquarters in England was written their motto, "Jehovah-Jireh."

I provide for My people, but notice My provision is based on *relationship*. Just as Abraham obeyed, so you must obey if you want My provision.

Abraham was surrendered to Me. He was willing to go where I led, and he ventured out not knowing where he was going. He began his journey with the attitude, "Here I am." *Pray: Lord, here I am to do Your will... lead me.*

Abraham followed Me on a three-day excursion. Abraham did not make a spur of the moment act of surrender to Me. Abraham had made that lifetime commitment. For Me to provide for you, you must also make a long-term commitment. *Pray: Lord, I will go where You lead me... provide for the journey.*

Abraham was asked to do one of the most difficult things in life. He was asked to sacrifice his dreams. Don't most fathers have great dreams for their son? Abraham was asked to sacrifice his love. And if Abraham's son whom he loved was gone, everything the patriarch valued in life would be destroyed. But Abraham received everything I promised him because he was willing to give up everything. *Pray: Lord, I give You everything; I give You my life.*

I Provide

YOUR TIME TO PRAY

*Lord, I trust my entire life to You,
I know You will protect me
And You will provide what You promise.
I surrender my dreams to You,
Take me and use me according to Your will.
Lord, I worship You as Jehovah-Jireh.
I wait silently in Your presence.
Amen.*

24

I PROTECT

> *If you diligently heed My voice, the LORD your God and do what is right in My sight, give ear to My commandments and keep all My statues, then I will protect you from the diseases I put on the Egyptians. For I am your Lord (Jehovah Rapha), who heals you.* —Exodus 15:26 ELT

In the Bible, you can see that I am concerned about your health and healing. I the Lord can heal you in two ways. First and primary by preventative healing, which is keeping disease and bacteria from inflecting you. This is called My protective shield from sickness and diseases. *I protect.* Second, through curative medicine that makes you well or My miraculous healing power. I can heal you. Either way you can pray for Me to actively heal you.

In a small way, a mother protects her children. To prevent her child from getting sick, a mother will make sure the home is clean, disinfecting and getting rid of as many germs as possible. She'll make sure her child gets well-balanced, healthy meals. When cold weather, she will make sure the child is dressed properly. And oh, don't forget the shots. She makes sure her child is vaccinated. This is her protective healing.

But you live in a germ-infected world, and most every child will catch a cold or virus. That's where curative medicine comes in. A loving mother takes the child's temperature and spoons out medicine. She phones the doctor and makes sure her child gets the proper treatment. She makes sure the child gets rest and sleep. She does everything to cure the illness and make the child well.

Just like the mother, I have compassion for My children. I want you to live healthy lives of worship and service. I never planned to save the souls of My children and neglect their physical bodies.

I want My people to be holy, which involves being clean in their speech, their clothing, and their bodies. So I instruct My children how to live, and those who obey My instruction are kept from many of the diseases that attack the body. My instructive care, both positive and negative, represents My protection of My children.

When Christians said they wouldn't smoke tobacco products, many laughed at them, accusing Christians of being legalistic or judgmental. But medical research later proved that smoking leads to lung cancer and other diseases. Since the body of a believer is the temple of the Holy Spirit, I want the body clean because I live in the believer. So, separation from sin has proven to be My preventative healing.

The same is true with drinking alcohol to get drunk. I want My people to be in control of their mental and physical faculties; and when they get drunk, they lose control. Also, alcohol consumption can lead to cirrhosis of the liver, hardening of the arteries, and a host of other diseases. Shakespeare said, "He who fills his stomach with wine, destroys his mind."

Think of all the dietary restrictions I put upon My people in the wilderness. They couldn't eat certain reptiles, birds, or insects. They could not even eat fish without scales. I was not being arbitrary. All the living things they could not eat were scavenger animals. Think of all the germs in a dead carcass or the bacteria found in a garbage dump. Some of the prohibited animals ate the highly germ-infested feces of other animals. I didn't want My people to put an animal into their bodies that was filled with germs and poison. The animals they could eat were vegetarians.

Even My rule of sexual purity, abstinence, prevented disease. There is a worldwide epidemic of AIDS and its corollary diseases. Governments are spending billions to find a cure for this deadly disease, but AIDS could be mostly wiped out if every man and woman obeyed My command, "Thou shalt not commit adultery" (Exod. 20:14). *Pray: Lord, I will be sexually pure; be glorified in my body.*

You serve Me the Lord *Jehovah Rapha*--the One who heals. I bless your life with preventative medicine; but to be healthy, you have a responsibility to "listen to My voice, I am the LORD your God" (Exod. 15:26). More than just knowing My rules for healthy living, you must, "keep all of My principles" (Exod. 15:26 ELT).

When you know Me and love Me with all your heart, then you will want to please Me in every area of your life. You want to be holy in your thoughts, and holy in your emotions. When you are holy and clean in your inner life, it's only natural you'll be holy in your outward physical life.

So, live a life of worship. Just as the Old Testament saints worshipped Me by bringing a lamb in sacrificial worship, so you can worship Me with a living sacrifice. The Bible instructs you how to do this. "I beseech you therefore, brethren, by the mercies of God, that you present your bodies a living sacrifice, holy, acceptable to God, which is your reasonable service" (Rom. 12:1).

Your holiness—cleanliness—is worship to Me.

By worshipping Me with your body, you are taking steps to preventative health. You allow Me to be *Jehovah Rapha* to you.

I Protect

YOUR TIME TO PRAY

Lord, forgive me when I complain about Your commands;
Sometimes I think I know better than You.
Help me see Your big picture You have for my life,
For my inward holiness and outward health.
Forgive me when I disobey Your commands,
And sin in either my heart or with my body.
Protect me from disease that attacks my body;
Heal me, make me healthy to serve You.
Lord, I offer my body to worship You.
Thank You for Your wise commands to make me healthy.
Amen.

25

I CAN BE PLEASED

> But without faith it is impossible to please Him, for he who comes to God must believe that **He is,** and that He is a rewarder of those who diligently seek Him. —Hebrews 11:6

Napoleon's French army had invaded a remote island in the Mediterranean Sea. Resistance was fierce and there was a large loss of life on both sides. Finally, the island was secure, and all resistance was wiped out.

According to Napoleon's custom, a large banquet was thrown for his officers to reward those with outstanding accomplishments in battle. Each officer nominated his troops for bravery or great accomplishments; but of course, Napoleon himself decided who would get rewards.

After the rewards were handed out, everyone settled into eating, drinking, and merriment. It was then that a young lieutenant approached Napoleon, snapped to attention and saluted.

"What do you want?" Napoleon returned the salute.

The room got deathly silent. All the other officers were appalled that a lowly lieutenant would approach the most successful general in all of Europe. For such impotence, other lowly officers had been demoted or confined to their quarters. Silence imprisoned the room.

I Can Be Pleased

"'What do you want?' Napoleon repeated his question.

"Sir," the lieutenant replied, standing motionless, "give me this island. It's my boyhood home!"

The room of officers was aghast. Their incredulous unbelief publicly exploded.

Quickly, Napoleon asked for paper, turned his back to the room and scribbled something. Smiling, the general handed the young lieutenant the paper, and then announced to the room, "The island is his; that's a title deed."

Now the officers were even more bewildered. Dumbfounded, they looked to one another for an answer. They all wanted to ask the same question, "Why?" The second in command turned to Napoleon to ask, "We have lost many loyal French soldiers in the battle for this island. Why would you capture it to give it to a lowly lieutenant?"

Napoleon answered, "He honored me with the magnitude of his request."

Napoleon could have had any land he desired, and his army could have captured any that defied him. Napoleon realized that the young lieutenant had paid him the greatest compliment of all by realizing he had the military power to capture anything he desired and the political power to give it away. The young lieutenant realized Napoleon could do anything he wanted without asking anyone, and that pleased Napoleon.

That is the picture I want you to see of how your faith can honor Me when you ask for Me to do incredible things for you. If you want to please Me, you must have as much faith in Me your heavenly Father as the young lieutenant had in Napoleon, and more so.

You please Me when you totally believe that I exist. You please Me when you know that I am eternal, and you are here on earth for just a short time. You also bring Me joy when you acknowledge I am Creator of everything and gave My Son's life so you could be saved and live for

Me. *Pray: Lord, I know You exist, but sometimes I don't act like You're here. Forgive me!*

Faith may be the greatest of all the qualities a human can possess. Oh yes, faith, hope, and love remain, and Paul said the greatest was love (see 1 Cor. 13:13). Paul meant love was the greatest in influencing others. But your faith is the greatest all-time power because your faith can influence Me. While hope and love are aimed at influencing others. *Pray: Lord, I want to please You.*

A lot of people have asked Me for something big but didn't really believe I would or could give it to them. Those people didn't have faith. Some ask for really big things—like millions of dollars or for faith healing, or for some other huge request. But did they ask according to the rules of My Kingdom? Can you say you have faith in Me if you ask contrary to My rules? The same goes for those who ask ignorantly.

You please Me when you ask according to the way I instructed you. But if you have a shallow understanding of Me, you demonstrate your lack of attention of learning about Me and My ways. I reward according to your faith; not your audacity.

My Son Jesus explained this principle when He said, "Have faith in God" (Mark 11:22). Just recognize Me, do what I say, and you will please Me. And when I am pleased, you can boldly ask for big things, even moving mountains. "For assuredly, I say to you, whoever says to this mountain, 'Be removed and be cast into the sea,' and does not doubt in his heart, but believes that those things he says will be done, he will have whatever he says. Therefore, I say to you, whatever things you ask when you pray, believe that you receive them, and you will have them" (Mark 11:23-24).

Saying what you want is not the key to moving the mountains in your life. *Naming* it is not the key to *claiming* it. The key is your faith that pleases Me so that I reward you.

If there is a secret to faith, it's wrapped up in one word—*relationship*. You think you know your spouse when you stand before a preacher to get married, but it's really only just the beginning of a relationship. You'll know each other much more intimately after fifty years of marriage. In the same way, after living with Me for fifty years, you will know Me more intimately and be able to better please Me. If you believe I exist and I am worthy of one or two hours of time a day, you will please Me by spending that time with Me. And the more you know Me, the better your faith can honor Me with the magnitude of your request. That faith will move mountains as I reward you.

Reflect on My heart. Does your faith please Me daily or do you pretty much live your life to please yourself?

YOUR TIME TO PRAY

Lord, forgive me for spending so little time with You,
Forgive me for knowing so little about You;
I'm sorry I've not learned how to fully obey You.
Lord, I want to move mountains that block my life,
And I want my prayers answered,
But it's my lack of faith that hinders me.
Lord, I will go deep in Scripture to learn how You answer;
I will learn to know You and fellowship with You
So You will reward my faith for the magnitude of my requests.
Amen.

26

I ANGUISH

> *Then I came with My disciples into a garden called Gethsemane...then I said to them, "My soul is anguished even to death, wait and pray with Me." —Matthew 26:26,28 ELT*
>
> *And being in agony, I anguished in prayer, and great drops of blood, as sweat, fell to the ground. —Luke 22:44 ELT*

Shrouded by dark clouds looming in the east, the moon refused to show itself. The apostles struggled to distinguish the garden path by starlight.

"If the Master did not come here so often," one disciple said, "we would never find the garden in the darkness."

They knew the way because they often came with Me to pray in the Garden of Gethsemane. Now I strode toward the garden without a misstep, even as the apostles stumbled over stones and tree roots, unable to see the ground in front of them. Each disciple was lost in his own thoughts. My prediction that each of them would forsake Me before the night was through loomed in their minds.

The city of Jerusalem slept silently behind them. Water gurgled in the creek of Kidron below them. The April rains had freshened the springs, and the lapping brook was the only sound that broke the silence of darkness.

Off to their right appeared the vague silhouettes of a grove of olive trees. Their gnarled trunks made for excellent seats, so I directed the apostles, "Sit here," as they entered the garden. "I will go ahead to pray."

I took Peter, James, and John with Me, disappearing into the darkness. It was late in the evening, and the apostles were tired and growing cold. They wrapped their tunics about them to ward off the damp chill.

Deep in the garden, I spoke to My three closest disciples. "I am overwhelmed with grief," I said, "crushed almost to the point of death."

I instructed the three, "Stay here and keep watch with Me as I pray." But even as I walked away, the three men felt their eyes getting heavy and their shoulders sagged. Soon they were propped against the olive trees sleeping.

About a stone's throw away, I fell to My knees to pray. Visions of the cross bore down on Me; I knew the intense pain and agony that awaited Me on the morrow. I cried out to My heavenly Father as the darkness pressed in on My Spirit from all sides. *"My Father..."* the words poured out of My heart like water from a pitcher *"...if it is possible, I don't want to drink this cup of suffering."*

My agony was so intense that I could no longer remain on My knees. I fell with My face to the ground. My fists clenched. My voice tightened. I repeated My plea, *"Father, if You are willing, please take this cup from Me."*

The garden usually talked to Me at night. I often heard the hoot of an owl, the coo of a dove, the unusual whistle of the night birds. But tonight, silence surrounded Me. There wasn't even a breeze to rustle the leaves. The garden seemed stillborn.

Then off in the distance came a low rumble. A spring storm moved down the Jordan Valley. I did not see the lightning, but I heard the groan of heaven. One by one, the stars were extinguished by the fast-moving clouds. On My recent vigils in the garden, I had enjoyed the light of the moon and stars, but tonight heaven seemed shut up.

"*Why?*" My heart cried out.

Disturbed by the distant thunder, I rose and returned to where I had left Peter, James, and John. They were sleeping soundly. I knew the weakness of being physically tired but was disappointed that their professed love for Me had not driven them to pray. I shook Peter's shoulder to ask, "Could you men not stay awake and keep watch with Me for even one hour?"

The three were embarrassed and said nothing. Peter hung his head; John looked off into the distance.

"Keep alert," I warned them. "Watch and pray or temptation will overcome you." The need to continue in prayer overwhelmed Me, and I turned to walk away. Looking back, I said to them, "Your spirit is willing, but the flesh is weak. Watch and pray."

I returned once more to the spot where I had knelt and prayed, *"My Father, if it's not possible for this cup of suffering to be taken away unless I first drink it...then may Your will be done."*

I knew that in the morning there would be humiliation, pain, torture, and finally death by the worst form of execution possible. Yet I yielded to My Father's greater plan. I would have to go through the cross to get back to My home in heaven.

"*My Father,*" I continued to pray, "*My Father, why must I go through the cross?*" Each time I came to the same conclusion: *"Nevertheless, not My will, but Yours be done."*

I once again heard the sounds of snoring and went again to My disciples, finding them sound asleep. "Why can't you keep your eyes open?" I asked, but none of them moved.

Again, I was overcome with anguish. I walked away from those whom I called "friends." Lesser men had faced execution without a whimper, but lesser men did not wrestle for the souls of mankind. Lesser men did not understand what it meant to suffer the wrath of God the Father.

Again, collapsing under the load of grief, I fell to the ground. Clutching My fists and tightening My every muscle. Drops of blood beaded on My forehead, running down into My beard.

Perspiration dampened My whole body as I prayed with ferocity unknown to any human before or since. My face appeared to have been bloodied by an opponent.

My adversary, satan, gloated over My prostrate form, certain that ultimate victory was at hand. Then an angel from heaven came to Me and renewed My strength, and satan withdrew for the moment.

After a time, I gathered Myself and returned to My three most trusted disciples, the three who loved Me most. They were asleep.[1]

"Anguished" is a terrible word to describe excruciating or agonizing pain in both body and soul. I suffered acutely when I mentally faced the sufferings of the cross. My anguish began in My soul and slowly trickled throughout My being. *Pray: Lord, thank You for anguishing because of my sin.*

Can I Almighty God anguish? A smart person can usually get out of suffering. A rich man can buy his way out of most pain. Why did I your God anguish over the prospect of the cross?

Because only I knew the terrible nature of sin, while you are blinded by it. Only I your God knew the fierceness of My judgement, while you rationalize it away. Only I your God knew the torture of hell, and I anguished over the punishment of hell for you. *Pray: Lord, open my eyes to see the terribleness of sin.*

Since I anguished so much for you, how can you not give Me your service and worship? Why can you not do everything for Me?

YOUR TIME TO PRAY

Lord, I don't like to suffer anything physically,
And I hate any emotional or mental suffering.
Yet You went through the mental anguish of the cross,
Only hours before the physical suffering of Calvary.
Lord, thank You for Your sacrifice and courage.
Thank You for all the anguish You endured for me.
May I be willing to suffer for You
When persecution comes to me.
Amen.

NOTE

1. Adapted from Elmer Towns, *The Son* (Ventura, CA: Regal Books, 1999), 265-267. See Matthew 26:36-56; Mark 14:32-52; Luke 22:40-53; John 18:1-11.

I COLLECT TEARS IN A BOTTLE

> ...*Put my tears into Your bottle; are they not in Your book?*
> —Psalm 56:8

Elmer Towns used to keep things in old quart milk bottles. Early bottles were round, but later someone discovered they could store more bottles together if they were square. So, his later milk bottles were square.

He kept pennies in his milk bottle, but he never filled it up. Because he was poor, money burned a hole in his pocket, so he would spend his pennies long before the bottle was filled.

He used to play marbles and kept his marbles in a milk bottle, watching them sparkle in the rays of the sun. Elmer remembers knuckles down and his favorite shooter.

Why did he keep things in a milk bottle? Because he was a collector, and when his things were in a bottle—not a box—he could easily count to see how much he had collected.

Also, because Elmer was poor, he valued himself by how much he collected. So, he got some self-identity from collecting things. He would say to his buddies, "Look how many marbles I've got." Then they would compare collections. It was important to Elmer not to be embarrassed by someone's much larger collection.

Do you think I am a collector? What things would I collect? Maybe I collect things for the same reason you do. Now I would not have the same selfish motivation as humans. But the opposite might be true; you might have pure motivation you got from Me.

The opening verse to this study from Psalm 56 tells you that I have a bottle in heaven where I collect the tears of My followers. Was it an actual bottle or was it a metaphorical bottle that reflected My concern for you? In the Old Testament a bottle probably referred to a leather water skin; later in the New Testament, bottles were more likely to be glass. Do you think I have an actual bottle? How big is it?

My bottle mentioned in this passage tells of the fear of David when captured by the Philistines in Gad. David had been running from Saul who tried to kill him when his life-long enemies the Philistines got him. Notice the anguish of David's prayers: "Man would swallow me up," (Ps. 56:1 KJV) moaned David. He complained to Me, "My enemies would hound me all day" (Ps. 56:2). David told Me "[my enemies] twist my words" (Ps. 56:5). Therefore, in deep anguish and tears, David prayed to Me to "put my tears into Your bottle" (Ps. 56:8).

Did you notice the bottle was called "Your bottle?" I have My own bottle. I do not need your bottle, nor do I need to borrow one from someone else. I already have My bottle, so I did not need to create one or to use human ingenuity to make one. I have My own private bottle to hold your tears. *Pray: God, do You have any of my tears in Your bottle?*

You keep things precious to you in your bottle. What is precious to Me that I would keep in My bottle? Surely not the money you give to Me in the church offering plate, or the receipts for spending money on My causes. Surely, I do not keep your blue ribbons or first place trophies surrounding My bottle. I have tears in My bottle because they mean so much to Me.

Why your tears? Because your tears represent your most honest sincerity. You cry when you hurt the most. And when you pray from your deepest wounds and hurts, you pray best.

Also, you cry when you have lost all pride and self-image. When you do not care what people think of you, you hold back nothing. Tears make you genuine. *Pray: Lord, I will pray sincerely.*

I want to keep things that are genuine. Don't art dealers want the genuine painting for their collection? They don't want a copy or a forgery. The same is true with Me. I want to remember the times in your life when you were more honest than any other time.

David was being completely honest with Me his Lord when he penned the words to Psalm 56. I had anointed him king over Israel, and young David knew it. David had killed Goliath when Saul wouldn't go to battle. Then Saul became jealous of David and tried to kill him. My enemies—the Philistines—probably hadn't forgotten that David killed Goliath, their champion. Now the Philistines had David in their grasp. No wonder David was scared. He was probably more scared than when he faced Goliath. He was probably more scared than any time in his life. So, David prayed honestly, sincerely, and with genuine faith——so genuine that he wept with tears. I wanted to collect and keep his tears in a bottle.

In addition to storing David's tears in the bottle, Psalm 56:8 also tells you that I had a book. It could have been a book where I kept a record of what went into the bottle. I wrote down when David cried, where David cried, and why David cried.

For all you know, My book could have included a ranking of all the tears of David that were in My bottle. Humans measure on a scale of 1 to 10. Would they have measured this time when David prayed when he was captured by the Philistines as a 10—and all other tears were a 9 or below?

I do not rank your tears in a book. But there is a book of works that will be opened in the future judgment (see Rev. 20:12-15). I know the sincerity of every prayer you have ever prayed, and every work you have ever done. I will reward you accordingly.

It's all right to weep, because My Son Jesus wept (see Chapter 29), and it's all right to laugh because Jesus laughed (see Chapter 18). The Bible teaches "A time to weep and a time to laugh" (Eccles. 3:4).

So, weep in prayer for your unsaved relatives and friends to be saved. Remember, the one "Who continually goes forth weeping, bearing seed for sowing, shall doubtless come again with rejoicing, bringing his sheaves with him" (Ps. 126:6). Do you see weeping and laughing?

Also, there is a time to weep when you fully face your sins. A fallen woman came behind Jesus, "And stood at His feet behind Him weeping" (Luke 7:38). What good did her tears do? I saw her tears and knew her sincerity. I said, "Her sins, which are many, are forgiven; for she loved much" (Luke 7:47). Pray: *Lord, my sins are many; forgive me.*

So, if you've been weeping, remember your tears are precious to Me. They are remembered in a bottle. But look beyond your tears for "weeping may endure for a night, but joy comes in the morning" (Ps. 30:5).

YOUR TIME TO PRAY

Lord, You see my tears when I pray
Sincerely from the depths of my soul,
May my tears tell You of my love for You.
I plead Your mercy and love,
Forgive my sin and cleanse me of every transgression
Accept me back into Your fellowship.
But I want more...
I want to feel the acceptance of Your presence.
Amen.

28

I HAVE UNKNOWABLE SECRETS

> *And Abraham planted a grove of trees on the edge of the desert at the seven springs of Beersheba (the wells where an oath was promised), and Abraham called on the name of El Olam (the eternal hidden God).* —Genesis 21:33 ELT

Elmer Towns' wife, Ruth, was 31 years old when she found out the secret of all secrets about her life. She found out her mother and father were not her biological parents, she was adopted. Discovering that secret of her birth was so transforming that it shook her inwardly. She was not the physical child of Elvira and Elton Forbes; they adopted her when she was two months old. Finding out that she was not her mother's daughter finally explained some of the many differences between her and her adoptive parents.

Finding out a secret released some powerful forces in Ruth. She had to ask, "Who am I?" and she was free from the biological necessities or restraints of her adoptive parents. Since she did not know—and since has not found out—who her parents were, she was free to become who she wanted to be. She no longer had to be like her adoptive parents.

Did you know I your God have secrets?

UNDERSTANDING THE PERSON OF GOD

It has to do with My name when I was first called *El Olam* at the Oasis at Beersheba. The name *Olam* meant I was eternal or "from everlasting to everlasting, I am God" (Ps. 90:2 ELT). But My name *Olam* has a second deeper meaning, "the things forever kept secret." It carries the meaning I your God hides, or I your God am hiding My identity so that I will not be understood by humans. It is not that I try to hide things from you, but you as a human just cannot understand all that I your God am like. Therefore, there is a part of Me that you can never understand.

You can only know the things about Me that I reveal to you, and I do not always choose to reveal everything about Myself to you.

Ruth's parents did not tell her she was adopted because there was a pervasive belief in their day that she would not understand or she would not love her adopted parents if she found out she was adopted.

But that is not right. Ruth found herself loving her parents more because they picked her and voluntarily sacrificed for her. Ruth felt special because she was chosen, whereas birth parents don't have a choice with the child they receive.

In Genesis 21, Abraham first called Me *El Olam*. In the story, Abraham and his family had traveled to a place called Gerar, where a man named Abimelech was king. The king wanted to make a treaty with Abraham, so he asked Abraham to swear before God that he would not deal falsely with him or any of his descendants. Abraham agreed, but he went on to complain to Abimelech that some of his shepherds who had worked for Abraham had dug some wells at Beersheba in the flat sandy desert of south Israel. But the shepherds of Abimelech had violently taken them away. This was perhaps done because the Philistines thought the south desert belonged to them and not Abraham. They treated Abraham as a trespasser (see Gen. 21:22-26). Before Abimelech and Abraham agreed, Abraham brought out seven lambs as a gift to Abimelech, apparently to "buy" the wells so he could live there: "Thus they made a covenant at Beersheba" (Gen. 21:32).

After Abimelech left, Abraham worshipped Me his Lord, *El Olam*. There were probably a lot of things Abraham didn't understand about Me. Perhaps he did not understand how I would eventually give him the entire Promised Land. Perhaps he did not understand how the fear of Me gripped Abimelech's heart. Could this well be My down payment to Abraham for the Promised Land, as though I was saying, "I'm giving you the title deed to the well of Beersheba as proof that I will later give you the entire Promised Land"?

This book is about finding and encountering My heart. But this chapter is about the things that I won't reveal, and you can't know. These are some secrets I do not tell you about. If I did, it might overwhelm you, scare you, or paralyze you. *Pray: Lord, thank You for not telling me everything about Yourself. I am too human to understand.*

Suppose you knew whom you should marry from infancy. Suppose you knew the day you would die. If you knew these things, they would not be kept secret from you, you would miss out on the experiences and growth that would make you into the person I want you to be. You would never grow to become what I want you to be if there was no mystery, no challenge, and no threats.

When I do reveal Myself to you, it has a purpose. I have said, "The secret things belong to the Lord your God, but those things which are revealed belong to you and to your children forever, that you may do all the words of this law" (Deut. 29:29 ELT). Did you notice why I show you certain things? It is so you may benefit from them and obey them. *Pray: Lord, help me respond correctly to everything You reveal to me.*

You must worship *El Olam* for who I am and for what I do. I *El Olam* may not do things the way you do them, and you cannot always understand Me: "For My thoughts are not your thoughts, nor are your ways My ways." When you do not understand, it is important to remember that when your vision is limited and small, My vision is perfect and eternal. I view the big picture; I see the grand plan. "For as the heavens are higher than the earth, so are My ways higher than your ways, and My thoughts than your thoughts" (Isa. 55:8-9). *Pray: Lord, I accept Your thoughts to rule my life, and Your way of doing things.*

You can learn a wise lesson from Abraham: when Abraham could not understand what I was doing in his life, he stopped to worship Me, *El Olam.*

YOUR TIME TO PRAY

Lord, I pause to worship You for Your work
In my life and family today.
Lord, I don't always understand what You are doing
And at times I resist Your plans and purposes.
Forgive me for my selfish struggles against You,
Teach me to trust You when I can't see
What You are doing in my life.
I want You to lead me and give me
The best You want me to have.
Amen.

29

I DON'T TELL EVERYTHING

> *However, no one knows the day or hour when these things will happen, not even the angels in heaven or the Son himself. Only the Father knows.* —Matthew 24:36 NLT
>
> *The LORD our God has secrets known to no one. We are not accountable for them, but we and our children are accountable forever for all that he has revealed to us, so that we may obey all the terms of these instructions.*
> —Deuteronomy 29:29 NLT

I am the Lord of eternity and God of creation. I know everything that is knowable, but I also know all the things that could have occurred but didn't. That means I know every thought in the mind of all people, of all time; as well as I know all the potential things that could have happened but didn't; and I know all the potential thoughts that all people could have thought, but didn't.

But at the same time, I don't tell you or any human all that I know, or all that I plan, or all that has the potential of happening in your life or all lives. That means I have secrets.

UNDERSTANDING THE PERSON OF GOD

When My Son Jesus was on earth, He prophesied about His future return at the end of time. He also predicted many of the events and trends that would occur when He returned. But in His earthy body, Jesus was totally God—deity—and at the same time totally human, with a perfect but limited human nature. In His humanity on earth, He didn't know the time He would return in His rapture, or glorious manifestations.

He didn't know because He didn't need to know. Things were happening around Him on earth He didn't know. Remember the woman in the crowd who touched Him, but He didn't know who it was? He asked, "Who touched My clothes?" (Mark 5:30). But I His heavenly Father told Him all He needed to know, when He needed to know. So, humans today don't know when Jesus will return to earth.

If humans knew when Jesus' return would take place, they would repent for the wrong reason. I know that decision would not lead to salvation because people weren't choosing to be disciples of My Son—their empty conversion would be a result of fear, or any other motive. True conversion is when people repent of sin because the Holy Spirit convicts them, they voluntary choose to follow Jesus out of a love and the accept the propitiation of Jesus' death on the cross for forgiveness of sin. Because I know everything in the hearts of all people, I know when they seek salvation. So, I withhold from all people their knowledge of the time and date of Jesus' return to earth.

All you know about the coming rapture of believers and the return of My Son to earth is that it will happen imminently—at any given time, on any given day, throughout time. Jesus could have returned 1,000 years ago, or it could not happen until a future date 1,000 years from now. But as the Scriptures explain, "The LORD our God has secrets known to no one." Why? "...that we may obey all the...instructions" (Deut. 29:29 NLT).

Let's move your thinking from the Second Coming to everyday decisions that I don't tell; I keep secrets. Again, there are divine reasons why I don't tell you everything that will happen to you. If you know all the good

I Don't Tell Everything

things that are in your future, and the problems, pain, and pressures, you would not face them properly. The good things you may anticipate and plan for them your way. If you know about the pain and disappointment, you may not face them by faith, and you may plan to act differently—you might even let your sin nature control you. Because you don't know your future, you must trust Me completely to guide you. Then you will find all things will, "work together for good to those who love God" (Rom. 8:28). *Pray: Lord, I trust Your timing to tell me things when I need to know. And I trust Your timing to tell me things I should not know.*

In another chapter in this book I stated, "I have a plan for your life" (Jer. 29:11). That is because, I plan. Because I am good, My plan is "to do good things for you and not to harm you" (Jer. 29:11). Sometimes it may be good for you to suffer persecution for your faith or suffer physical pain, also within My plan for all people.

Now your walk with Christ and your testimony to both saved and unsaved is more important in My plan for your life than your physical freedom from pain and your earthly pleasures. Your obedient faith means more to Me than anything else.

YOUR TIME TO PRAY

Lord, I have learned positive lessons from hard times.
I am glad I did not know about them before they came.
I might have acted differently and missed
The positive lessons and Your good blessings.
I am glad You have a plan for my life,
I submit to Your guidance and anticipate Your blessings.
Amen.

30

I GET ANGRY

> *I the Lord will avenge in fury, I will take vengeance on My adversaries, and I reserve wrath for My enemies, but I am slow to anger.* —Nahum 1:2-3 ELT

A young single mom was perpetually angry. Her husband divorced her because she always fussed at him. She was mad at life because she got stuck with a baby. She barely got through high school, hated to study, and never acquired a skill for a job. She ended up as a maid, cleaning motel rooms. She hated her job, as evidenced by her messy apartment that smelled because she never cleaned it up.

Her bank card and department store bills were several months delinquent. The collection agency phoned over and over again about overdue bills. When one creditor threatened further action, she mailed a check for more than $400 to satisfy the immediate problem. However, the creditor phoned her again because the store never received the check.

The single mother went into a rage. She insisted the store was "dumb" for losing her check and blamed the store for not hiring enough people to take care of business correctly.

When the agent on the phone asked if she had mailed the check after writing it, she yelled at him again. He tactfully suggested that she might have lost the envelope. He asked her to look in the drawer where she kept her bills or in her purse.

The woman continued to yell. Next, she blamed the post office. Now she was angry at the post office for not delivering the check to the store! Eventually, she settled down long enough to call her bank and cancel the check. Still griping and complaining, she mailed the second check for the balance to the store.

Everyone who knew the single mom knew her anger was destroying her life, financially, socially and emotionally, but the woman continued to rage on, unaware of the vast impact her anger was having on her life.

Did you know that I your God get angry? I have standards of holiness and when people break My laws or principles, I become angry at their sin. So if I get angry, it must be all right for you to get angry. Yes—but you must get angry at the right things and for the right reasons. It's wrong to get angry at the wrong person or for the wrong reason. The woman in the illustration was angry for the wrong reason and angry at the wrong people. The Bible instructs, "Be angry, and do not sin" (Eph. 4:26). This verse allows you to be angry, but it warns you not to sin with your anger.

You get your anger from Me because you are made in My image, which means you have a personality like Mine. You have intellect, emotion, and will, which is the power of choice. In the perfect world, only the things that anger Me should anger you, but you are a fallen, sinful being and so your anger often is expressed in inappropriate ways and times. I gave you the Ten Commandments to tell you how to live. The order of the ten laws reflects their importance. The first commandment tells you to have no gods before Me. The second commandment tells you not to have any carved idols. Those who bow down to idols are warned, "I, the LORD your God, am a jealous God, visiting the iniquity of the fathers on the children to the third and fourth generations of those who hate

Me" (Exod. 20:5). Did you see why I get angry? Those who worship an idol instead of Me, actually hate Me.

Because I created you and you belong to Me, you make Me angry when you refuse to recognize My lordship over you. I get angry when you put something in My place. *Pray: Lord, I put You first in my life.*

Compare My anger to the illustration of the single mom's anger. I show My anger only at the right time, for the right reason. I do not walk around angry at every person. In contrast, the single mom was angry at everyone and blamed everyone for her problems.

Though I get angry, I do not always act on it. I control My anger. The Bible says, "The LORD is slow to anger" (Nahum 1:3). If I instantly punished everyone who broke My law, no one would live; all would be eliminated. *Pray: Lord, thank You for Your patience with me.*

What holds Me back from immediately punishing every sin and every sinner? It's My everlasting love for people. I am able to control My anger because of My compassion.

Perhaps the single mom has never truly experienced love. Maybe she's never been loved, so she is not able to love others. Maybe she's angry because no one cares for her or protects her from the uncertainties of life.

Remember, I love you and have a wonderful plan for your life. As I progressively lead you, I am showing you My love. So, find My plan for your life, then live it and do it. *Pray: Lord, show me Your plan for my life.*

YOUR TIME TO PRAY

Lord, sometimes I'm angry at the wrong person
For the wrong reason; forgive me.
Help me control my temper and anger;
Give me the Holy Spirit's power to do it.
Lord, transform me by Your power;
I want to live like Christ.
Amen.

31

I HATE CERTAIN THINGS

> *These six (things) I the LORD hate, yes, seven (are) an abomination to Me. A proud look, a lying tongue, hands that shed innocent blood, a heart that devises wicked plans, feet that are swift in running to evil, a false witness (who) speaks lies, and one who sows discord among brethren.*
> —Proverbs 6:16-19 ELT

You often hear about My love, but I am capable of hate too. Look again at the verse from Proverbs that lists what I hate. First, a proud look. Certain people have a selfish glow when they are pleased with themselves, or they have gained mastery of others. Their world is wrapped up in themselves.

The second thing I hate is a lying tongue, and the third thing are hands that shed innocent blood.

The fourth thing is people with wicked dreams and imaginations because those people usually act out dreams they imagine.

The fifth thing I hate are feet that are quick to run to do mischief. The mischief referred to here is harm to people.

The sixth thing that I hate is a proud heart that becomes a false witness who spreads lies. Most selfish people are blind to the good things of others. They exalt themselves and believe the lies they tell about themselves. Then they put others down and believe the lies and rumors they spread about others.

The seventh thing I hate is sowing discord among other Christians. If you love other people, you wouldn't spread rumors that destroy them.

These seven things that I hate deal with inward sins of the heart, not outward sins. Your inward motives always determine your outward actions, your inward selfish pride is the source of your sin that I hate.

Notice that your selfishness is the basis for several issues such as pride, false witnesses, lies, and sowing discord among friends. When a man or woman is all bound up in their selfish lifestyle, they can't worship or serve Me their Lord. These are things that get in the way of worship.

Most don't like selfish individuals. Who wants to listen to people who always talk about themselves—their own accomplishments, possessions, looks, clothes, and what they do to have fun?

It's not wrong to talk about your accomplishments, if you do it at the right time for the right reason. And it's not wrong to be concerned about your clothes and the way you dress. There is a place for self-love. Which begins with proper self-respect. Remember, the Great Commandant, "You shall love the LORD your God with all your heart...soul, and...mind" (Matt. 22:37-38). Don't forget the second part, "You shall love your neighbor as yourself" (Matt. 22:39). Did you see that part about "love yourself?" I recognize your self-love.

I know it is natural for people to love themselves, or I wouldn't have added, "as you love yourself." So how is it all right to love oneself? Again, let's call it "self-respect." You must know yourself for who you are. It's all right to feel the satisfaction of accomplishment when you do well. It's wrong to brag about your accomplishments that are greater than they really are. That's lying, or worse, self-worship. That's where the ego comes in; that's where sin influences you.

It's not wrong to love yourself with proper self-worth or self-respect. If you exaggerate your self-worth, that's pride. But if you minimize your self-worth, you create low self-esteem. So, what's a healthy ego or a proper self-esteem? It's when you know yourself for who you are. It's when you don't exaggerate or diminish your self-worth. It's when you are honest with yourself.

I announced the Kingdom of heaven was a spiritual kingdom where I desired to sit on the throne of your heart, to rule your life. Who controls your heart and life? *Pray: Lord, sit on the throne of my life, "Not I but Christ."*

When selfish pride sits on the throne of your life, I am displaced. You can't call Me Lord and give Me second place in your life. *Pray: Lord, come now, control my life.*

Let's not end this chapter on a negative note. Look again at My love that is everlasting and My mercy that forgives every sin your selfish pride conceives. Praise Me for the cross, for that's where My blood was poured out to forgive your sin. *Pray: Lord, thank You for Your grace and mercy You poured on me through the cross.*

YOUR TIME TO PRAY

Lord, thank You that in mercy You forgave me;
I claim Your cleansing by My blood.
Forgive me for my pride and selfish acts,
That exalted me and not You.
Lord, make me be honest about myself
And my accomplishments.
I will exalt You in all I do,
Then I won't have trouble with pride.
Amen.

32

I PUNISH SIN

> *He had looked around at them with anger, being grieved by the hardness of their hearts....* —Mark 3:5

My disciples and I stood at the golden gate to Herod's temple. It was a beautiful, warm spring day in AD 26. The temple was crowded as people were preparing for Passover, the holiest day of the year.

When they entered the temple, however, My face fell. The disciples were worried. They had expected Me to show excitement coming to My Father's house; after all, they believed I was the Messiah who would drive the Romans into the sea and set up David's throne right there in Jerusalem. The disciples expected a great announcement, spectacular miracles, or some enormous divine appearance. But instead they saw My frown of disapproval.

"Why does Jesus look like He's angry?" one disciple asked another. Then they looked into the temple and were shocked at what they saw.

I had expected to hear the Levitical choir singing praise psalms or see people in worshipful meditation, but instead the temple sounded like a market bazaar. I heard people bargaining over prices and shopping for the cheapest sacrifice. At a table, customers and moneychangers were arguing over the exchange rate. Children were chattering and a donkey brayed.

I Punish Sin

When I could take it no longer, I shouted to the crowd, "MAKE NOT MY FATHER'S HOUSE A MARKET PLACE!"

I turned over the tables of moneychangers, yelling at them, "OUT!" I pointed to the East Gate. "LEAVE IMMEDIATELY!"

The crowd was too shocked to reply. They watched with wonder as I moved from table to table, scattering coins on the stone pavement. Children laughed with glee as they chased coins rolling in every direction.

Then I twisted some ropes together to lay stripes on an ox. It bolted toward the temple gate with its owner running to retrieve his merchandise. The crowd laughed.

The crowd didn't yell at Me, nor did anyone try to stop Me. The Holy Spirit froze them in terror. There was enough God-consciousness left in them to tell them they were wrong. I the Father felt the same anger as My Son. I first entered the temple in the Shekinah cloud when Solomon prayed to dedicate the temple. The inhabitants worshipped in a holy hush. But a holy hush was not present in the temple that day; instead there was a carnival atmosphere. Then the crowd heard Jesus shout, "MY FATHER'S HOUSE IS A HOUSE OF PRAYER; YOU HAVE MADE IT A DEN OF THIEVES."

The disciples didn't help Me turn over the moneychangers' tables, nor did they drive out any of the sacrificial animals. They were riveted by My angry explosion. Everything they had experienced about Me had been kind and loving. But this...

One disciple quoted Psalm 69 in his attempt to understand what he saw: "My devotion to Your house, O God, burns in me like a fire" (John 2:17 Good News Translation).

Most think I am a loving Father, but this image of My Son's anger (found in Matthew 21:12-17, Mark 11:15-19, Luke 19:45-48, and John 2:13-16), goes against any modern perception of Me smiling and surrounded by children; My compassion in healing the multitudes. Yes, I am love, but I am also holy, which means I am separate from anything that

UNDERSTANDING THE PERSON OF GOD

is sinful or rebellious. To fully understand Me, you must realize I punish sin. I do it because I am angry with your sin.

Those who think I am only love and blessings have only seen one side of Me. The same is true of God the Father. Those who think I am a kind, genteel old grandfather have only seen one side of Me.

When a mother constantly tells her son to not touch a hot frying pan, and he continually reaches for it, what does she do? Does she let him touch the pan and possibly scar his hand forever? No! She spanks the hand to teach obedience and to protect her son. She doesn't spank to hurt her son, and she doesn't like to see him cry for the sake of tears.

What should I do when My children constantly disobey Me? If I looked the other way, I would deny the standards that reflect My nature. My anger at your disobedience is the other side of My love that protects you. I can let you scar yourself forever or I can correct you with a "pat" on the hand. My love takes over to correct and teach you. Sometimes in a punishing, correcting way.

But when you constantly disobey Me when you know better, then My anger is seen because I must discipline you.

When you stumble, I gently pick you up. When you ignorantly disobey Me and constantly turn your back on Me, what should you expect? I say, "My son, don't be angry when the Lord punishes you. ...When he whips you, it proves you are really his child" (Heb. 12:5-6 TLB). *Pray: Lord, I will be quick to obey You.*

I was angry because the priests who taught the Scriptures should have known better. They were housekeepers of My house, and they let it get dirty. They knew it was wrong to sell merchandise in My house, but they did it to make money. No wonder I was angry. *Pray: Lord, may I never do anything to get You angry at me.*

Have I ever been angry with you? Have you ever felt My stern rebuke? If so, repent immediately. Tell Me you're sorry. If tears don't come, maybe you have a hardened heart. Pray until I touch your heart. Then continue praying until you can touch Me.

YOUR TIME TO PRAY

Lord, I know You are a loving God;
I know You love me unconditionally.
But my sin breaks my fellowship with You,
Especially when I keep returning to the same sin.
No wonder You get angry with Your rebellious children.
Lord, I am sorry for my stupid selfishness;
I repent of my dumb disobedience.
Help me love You with all my heart;
Forgive me for my appetite for sin
And my neglect of Your standards of holiness.
Lord, don't be angry forever with me.
Look on my repentance with favor;
I want to always feel Your love.
Amen.

Section C

LEARNING THE MEANING OF MY BODY PARTS: MY SOURCE OF ACTION

Technically, I don't have body parts, just as I don't actually act physically (Section A) nor do I react physically (Section B). These are *anthropomorphisms*—projections of human body parts or activity onto Deity to help the reader understand the actions of the Divine.

In this section, My body parts are discussed to help you understand the source of My actions. Yes, I have a "mind" that does all the mental activity of a person. But I don't have a physical brain, the body organ where mental activity takes place.

When you read about My body parts, realize I know all about you, and I know the sources of your human activity.

33 – I Vomit

34 – I Turn My Back

35 – I Have a Face

36 – I Have a Mind

UNDERSTANDING THE PERSON OF GOD

37 – I Have a Heart

38 – I Have a Nose

39 – I Have Eyes

40 – I Have Wax in My Ears

41 – I Use My Fingers

33

I VOMIT

> *I know your works, that you are neither cold nor hot. I could wish you were cold or hot. So then, because you are lukewarm, and neither cold nor hot, I will vomit you out of My mouth.* —Revelation 3:15-16

Doesn't it sound strange that I the Lord God vomit? First let's look at the word "vomit." The dictionary explains, "To eject or disgorge the contents of the stomach through the mouth." "I can't stomach that," is a common expression today that describes vomiting without using the word. Vomiting is a polite way of describing your reaction to things or situations that are annoying, distasteful, or dangerous.

Second, let's examine why vomiting takes place? There are several reasons why people vomit. Sometimes it has to do with age, babies may spit up milk because it is sour, too cold, or some other reason. So when the milk doesn't digest, the baby spits it up or vomits it out. Sometimes older people have difficulty digesting certain foods, so they throw up.

Vomiting can happen because food is poison, or the stomach lining has a problem (gastritis), or there is an ulcer, or bulimia. Sometimes vomiting is the result of hormone problems, pregnancy, overeating, or motion sickness. Perhaps the person is sick with a stomach virus, diarrhea, cramps, abdominal pain, nausea, or dehydration. In addition, vomiting has many other causes described in medical journals.

The basic principle is that vomiting rids the body of unwanted, undesirable, or threating causes. Usually, vomiting is good because it rids the body of a major cause of bodily pain, preparing the body to heal itself.

Now why would I the Lord God who created the universe and human body, describe Myself as vomiting? Obviously, I am perfect and holy in all My nature, so nothing could contaminate Me, make Me sick, or in any way challenge my health. Remember, I your heavenly Father do not have a body, only Jesus My Son had a perfect body. He could not have been infected, nor could a disease invade His body.

But I used the human word "vomit" to describe My violent reaction to what displeases Me or violates My holiness. Just as a human body reacts to a threating substance and discharges it by vomiting, so I your Lord react to any threatening thing—whether substance, idea, influence, or human related—that is the opposite of My plan and will for humankind, or that is opposite to My holy nature.

The church at Laodicea was neither hot nor cold (Rev. 3:15). Their love for Christ did not move the thermometer. It was as though they never met Christ or followed Christ or did anything for Christ. Humans may say the Laodiceans were nonresponsive, or noncommitted. That may be the reason I rejected them. I reject those who do not follow Me or will not serve Me. Because they reject Me, I reject them. I display a human reaction, "vomit them out of My mouth." *Pray: Lord forgive me of all my known sins and my ignorant sins. May I be acceptable to You.*

But vomiting them out of My system is not the only thing. They will not enjoy My salvation, nor can they rest in my peace and the assurance I give to My followers that they not only know Me, but they also can look forward to living with Me at the rapture or death.

There is another result of being vomited out of My system. They will be judged at the Great White Throne Judgment, there to be cast into the Lake of Fire for eternity (Rev. 20:11-15).

Vomiting is a repulsive term because it describes a repulsive action of both humans and Me. But this violent term is only the beginning of My violent reaction to some people.

YOUR TIME TO PRAY

Vomiting is not a reaction someone choses to do.
It is usually an uncaused response to physical rejection.
I know God doesn't reject people because He wants to,
He rejects those who reject Him and rebel against Him.
Lord, I am not perfect, and I make mistakes,
But when my heart is not in response to Your love,
I know You will forgive me
When I admit my faults and plead forgiveness,
To be cleansed by the blood of Christ.
Amen.

34

I TURN MY BACK

> *As my glorious presence passes by, I will hide you in the crevice of the rock and cover you with my hand until I have passed by. Then I will remove my hand and let you see me from behind. But my face will not be seen.*
> —Exodus 33:22-23 NLT
>
> *My God, My God, why have You turned Your back on Me?*
> —Matthew 27:40 ELT

There are things I don't want to see, so the Bible describes Me as "turning My back." This is an anthromorphism, a human characteristic used to describe My back side. Technically, I see all things and know all things. So when My Son hung on the cross, I saw Him there; because I saw all the vicious torture done to Him, I did not want to see Him die. But when He became sin, your sin, I turned My back because I cannot look on sin.

Because I am holy, I cannot look on any rebellion, sin, or filthy things without reacting to it from My holiness. When I see sin, I punish or judge it instantly. When I see people sin, they may be punished by immediate consequences of its action, or I may arrange punishment in their earthly lives. But be assured, I will punish all persons and sin appearing before Me at the Great White Throne Judgment (Rev. 20:11-15).

My Son Jesus on the cross was no different. As a human father may want to avoid or stop any punishment on his son, I could not do that. Jesus became sin for all humans (1 Peter 3:18), so when I saw sin on My Son Jesus, I had to pour out My wrath and punishment on that sin. I did that as a holy God who also is just and righteous. I could not look on Jesus as a loving father looks on a son; I saw Him as He was, and I saw Him for what He became—the sin of the world.

Notice Jesus didn't address Me at that moment as "Father," for I was not in the role of a loving Father; Jesus called me "God," which described what I was doing, I was God judging sin.

So, there are two sides to My nature. On one side, I am love, and I love the world (John 3:16), and gave My Son to die for the world. But My other side is holiness, which demands, "I cannot look on sin."

What side of Me will face you after you die and appear before Me at the Great White Throne Judgment? Will I look on you in love because My Son Jesus died and suffered My punishment for your sins?

Or will you cry out when I must punish your sin, "Why have You turned your back on me?" Will you repeat the same words My Son said on the cross?

When you think of Me "turning My back," you see the nature of who I am. I am love who sent My Son to die for you. But I am also holy, and I cannot allow sin in My presence, or in My eternal home in heaven. *Pray: Lord, thank You for allowing Jesus to die for my sins.*

Today, as you read this explanation of My back side, and if you don't receive My Son as your Savoir, I will have to turn My love away from you. All you will see is My back side.

But if you will respond to My love, I will receive you to Myself, to My side. "For God so loved the world that He gave His only begotten Son, that whoever believes in Him should not perish but have everlasting life" (John 3:16).

YOUR TIME TO PRAY

Lord, I am not perfect, I know I have sinned,
Forgive me and cleanse me with the blood of Christ.
You turned Your back on Jesus on the cross,
Because He became my sin and died for me.
Now, I am as close to Your heart as Jesus,
Because He lives in me and I live in Him.
Amen.

35

I HAVE A FACE

> *"When I said, 'Seek My face,' your heart said, 'Your face, LORD will I seek...do not hide Your face from me'"*
> —Psalm 27:8-9 ELT

Until its collapse in 2003, the "Old Man of the Mountain," a rock formation that jutted out from Cannon Mountain, sat overlooking Profile Lake in New Hampshire. The Native American Indians who originally lived in the valley believed that the stone face represented a man who would come to the valley to bring much good for its inhabitants.

There is a story told about old stone face. A young boy sat for hours studying every feature of the stone face in the rock. The face in the cliff would look like the person who would come to do great things to the valley. The longer the boy memorized the features, the surer he became that he would be the first to recognize the stone face when he arrived.

One day a peddler came to town selling his wares, including his specialty, snake oil that promised to heal many diseases. The boy, believing that this was the man to bring good things, went running down Main Street telling everyone the stone face was coming. The peddler sold many bottles of his "healing oil" that day. However, the boy and the town soon realized that the oil did not hold any miraculous cure, and they became disillusioned.

Years later, another man came thought town selling shares to a promised railroad that would bring prosperity to the region. Again, the boy ran down the road yelling that stone face was coming. The man left town with the people's money, but the railroad never came. The boy became disillusioned again. "It is just a myth," he told himself.

Eventually the boy went off to college, and in the early colonial days, only churches began colleges. There a great revival occurred, and the boy became a Christian. God called the boy into ministry, and so the boy went back to his hometown to tell them the good news of Jesus Christ.

The boy, now grown into a young man, greeted the blacksmith, but the blacksmith did not return his greetings. He only stared. The same thing happened when he greeted a woman hanging her wash on a line. Repeatedly, people did not speak, but stared at him, seemingly in disbelief.

At first, the young man thought they were against him because he would preach the gospel in his hometown.

But no—the people stared because they young man's face had grown into the likeness of the great stone face, and the boy was now the man in the stone face. He had come to bring goodness to the valley; he had come to preach Jesus to them.

The deeper truth: you become like the person you spend your life gazing upon.

I have a face and I have told you to "Seek My face" (Psalm 27:8).

Because I am holy, when you meditate on Me, you will slowly become holy like Me. I have a heart—a good heart—and the more you contemplate Me, the more your heart becomes like My heart. Therefore, I want you to spend time reflecting on Me so you will become like Me. *Pray: Lord, I will gaze on You in the Scriptures and spend time in prayer. Give me Your heart.*

I Have a Face

How do you get a heart like Mine? Solomon said in Proverbs, "As in water face reflects face" (Prov. 27:19 NASB). That means that when you look into water, you see an image of your face looking back at you. But when you look into My face, do you see Me looking back at you? Then you make corrections in your attitudes or actions according to what you see in My face and that process will make you become like Me. *Pray: O Lord, help me see You so I can become like You.*

There was only one man in Scripture who saw My face. The Bible recounts, "So the LORD spoke to Moses face to face" (Exod. 33:11). How did that happen? No one had ever done that before.

As Moses was praying, he asked, "Please, show me Your glory" (Exod. 33:18). I answered Moses, "You cannot see My face; for no man shall see Me, and live" (Exod. 33:20). This is a predicament. How can I say in Psalm 27:8, "Seek My face," at the same time saying, "No man shall see Me, and live?"

Take a closer look at Moses. Because of his integrity and ability to intercede, part of Moses' request was answered. I took Moses to the top of Mount Sinai, put him into a split rock, and allowed My glory to pass in front of him. Then to save Moses' life, I used My hand to cover Moses. As My glory passed away from Moses, I removed My hand and Moses saw My back side.

Moses saw what no human had ever seen.

When Moses came down from Mount Sinai, the people were terrified of him. "Now it was so, when Moses came down from Mount Sinai (and the two tables of the Testimony were in Moses' hands when he came down from the mountain), that Moses did not know that the skin of his face shone while he talked with Him" (Exod. 34:29). Moses had been in My presence and seen My glory. He became like Me, the Person he passionately desired to gaze upon.

For forty days, Moses had to put a veil over his face when he talked to people because "they were afraid to come near him" (Exod. 34:30).

UNDERSTANDING THE PERSON OF GOD

Moses was physically transformed being face to face with Me. He went to the top of Mount Sinai that was covered with My Shekinah glory cloud. I was actually there. Moses talked with Me audibly and heard My words.

But you are different. You come to Me spiritually. You cannot see the physical features of My face for I am Spirit (see John 4:23). But you can talk to Me in prayer. Your inner spirit can feel My presence, and you can know what I am saying to you. *Pray: Lord, I come.*

Plus, you have something Moses did not have—My Words written in Scripture. When you read My Words in the Bible, I am speaking to you. When you reflect on My heart, you experience My presence in prayer.

So, confess your sins and ask Me to forgive them by the blood of Jesus (1 John 1:9). "Hide Your face from my sins" (Ps. 51:9). For if I were to judge your sin, you could not stand before Me. But I will forgive your sin when you ask for cleansing by the blood of Christ.

Your next prayer, "Do not hide Your face from me" (Ps. 102:2). You want to experience My atmospheric presence to learn My ways. You need Me to open your eyes so you can learn from the Scriptures.

Then you want to be holy as I your Lord am holy. You want to know Me and get close to Me. You want to walk with Me and enjoy fellowship with Me. When I tell you to seek My face, that is possible and that is doable.

Finally, your prayer is to ask My full blessing on your life, family, and service. "Make Your face shine upon Your servant" (Ps. 119:135).

YOUR TIME TO PRAY

Lord, I am looking forward to seeing something in heaven,
Something I cannot see while here on earth.
Lord, I am looking forward to seeing something
You promised me in Your Word.
Lord, You have promised in Scripture,
"His servants shall worship Him.
They shall see His face..."
(Revelation 22:3-4 AMP).
Amen.

36

I HAVE A MIND

> *My wisdom is great as are My knowledge and riches! It is impossible for you to understand My decisions and My methods of doing things! Who among you can know the mind of Me your Lord? Who knows enough to be My counselor and guide?* —Romans 11:33-34 ELT

Elmer Towns walked away from the nursing home disillusioned. His good friend and colleague didn't recognize him and could not converse with him. He told his friend a joke they had enjoyed years earlier, and the friend did not recognize the ironic punch line. He did smile though when Elmer laughed at the joke.

When someone has Alzheimer's, it is as though they are locked in a dark room where they recognize no one, and you cannot break into their darkness to talk to them.

Their mind is like an old prison. Some prison cells were built with an inner wall that does not get any sunshine all day. Prisoners had to look across the hall, or out a window to see sun shining on outside trees. One prisoner who had sun in his window could angle a mirror across the hall so another could enjoy a little warmth from the sun. That is like a person with a clear mind who has to shine the sunshine of his understanding to another who is an Alzheimer's prisoner.

I Have a Mind

That is what you do when visiting a friend with Alzheimer's. You shine a little sunlight of their past life into their consciousness. And doesn't the warm sun feel good anytime you experience the chill of darkness?

What discouraged Elmer most about his friend was his darkened mind. He had a PhD from Harvard and a law degree from Princeton, perhaps the most brilliant mind Elmer had ever encountered. One time in a faculty meeting, a question came up about the meaning of an English word. More than twenty academics could not define the word, but Elmer's friend not only defined it, he also gave the root in German and quoted a sentence from the German poet Goethe using the word. Brilliant!

But now, his mind was filled with barren darkness.

Elmer was despondent, asking Me his God if this illness could had been prevented? Elmer even rationalized, "I would like to have his mind."

You must be careful when you ask why I do certain things. Only I understand My reasons for doing the things I do. "For who has known the mind of the LORD? Or who has become His counselor?" (Rom. 11:34).

Did you know that I your God have a mind?

You can lose your memory, but I cannot. I know all things eternally. I will not forget anything.

You can misinterpret facts or hold incorrect opinions, but I your God cannot be wrong. I know all things perfectly. I even know all potential outcomes and those things that might have happened, but did not.

You sometimes have difficulty reasoning out things that later seem so simple. Some things you never reason out at all. My mind is perfect. I never forget anything. I always know the consequences of all actions, and the solution to all problems.

You can corrupt your mind by feeding it false doctrine or believing propaganda. You can become gullible when you believe the lies people tell you. I cannot believe a lie because I am truth, and I know all things.

The first and greatest power of the mind is to know one's self. At the onset of adolescence, a teenager often asks the question, "Who am I?" Nevertheless, I know Myself perfectly, so I will not ask that question.

Besides the question "Who am I?" you face other questions, such as "Why am I here on this earth?" and "Where did I come from?" These are basic questions that every human needs to answer.

You cannot be childish with these questions, like the little boy who ran in the kitchen to ask his mother, "Where did I come from?" She did not know how to answer, so she took a moment to decide if her son needed an answer from the creation of Adam or an answer about the birds and bees. Then her son solved her dilemma. "Mikey comes from Milwaukee. I just wanted to know what city I came from."

The scientists tell you that you use only a small part of your brain. You could be much smarter if you gave yourself to investigation, learning, memorization, and constant review. You could solve more problems, answer more questions, and provide more help to yourself and others. You could improve your mind with effort, but most do not.

There are two problems here. First, you could grow your ability to use your mind, but most do not give attention to this area of their lives. You offer Me a mind that is only half developed or ill-prepared. *Pray: Lord, forgive my laziness—give me motivation to learn!*

Think of a carpenter's shop and you are the tools on a workbench. Which tool would I pick up to use? When I need a chisel, I would usually choose the sharpest. The same for a saw, drill, or knife. Are you keeping your mind sharp and prepared for Me? *Pray: Lord, I will sharpen my mind so You can better use me.*

Beyond being sharp, you must also keep your mind clean, just as tools must be clean to avoid rust and decay. A carpenter would not reach for a tool dirtied by a spilled liquid or garbage on the tool table. No, I would choose a clean tool. *Pray: Lord, I repent of evil and dirty thoughts. Clean my mind and make me clean.*

Sometimes a man is working upstairs and his wife calls him to hang a picture. The tool that he needs is not available; it is down in the basement. So, he grabs the most available tool. He will drive that nail with the heel of his shoe.

Sometimes I have a job to do, but the brilliant Christian PhD is not available nor is an educated preacher around. So, I use the most available Christian, perhaps uneducated, but available and ready to be used by Me. You never know when, where, or how I will use you or need you, so you should always be prepared. *Pray: Lord, I am ready, fill me with wisdom and power and use me.*

Earlier I said there were two problems about knowing. The first was your uneducated mind. That can be improved. Second, some just do not know Me or My principles of ministry. They do not understand My nature or what I wrote in the Bible. They do not understand My principles of ministry or how they should serve Me. *Pray: Lord, I will learn how to serve You. Use me according to my usability.*

Remember, you got your mind from Me. You can reason, remember, and learn because you received these abilities from Me your Creator God. While My mind is perfect, I do not need to learn. You however must continue to grow in your intellectual abilities.

Some Christians have not grown intellectually nor do they intend to sharpen their mind. They think that yielding to Me is enough. I will use them according to their usability. But yielded ignorance is still ignorance. *Pray: Lord, I will learn more every day. Give me a thirst to grow in every area of my mind and life.*

As you reflect on My heart, look in My Word—the Bible—to see My mind. Learn the power of intelligence and place your mind under My direction. *Pray: Lord, here is my mind and thoughts; use them for Your glory.*

YOUR TIME TO PRAY

Lord, forgive me for mental laziness and pride of ignorance;
Help me discipline my mind to know more about You,
And a passion to be used by You.
Lord, I want to be the best servant I can be.
I will learn as much as I can learn,
And know You as intimately as possible.
Lord, don't let me squander the good mind You've given me,
Or destroy it with sinful things.
Keep my mind sharp for Your service.
Amen.

37

I HAVE A HEART

And I the LORD smelled a soothing aroma. Then I said in My heart, "I will never again curse the ground for man's sake" —Genesis 8:21 ELT

I your LORD have sought for a man after My own heart. —1 Samuel 13:14 ELT

Did you know I have a heart? Not a physical organ like yours, but just as your heart is filled with love for your mother or a special uncle or aunt or your first sweetheart, so I have a heart that reaches out to those I love. I have a heart that directs all I do. Just as your heart overflows with love on the day of your wedding, so My heart overflows to you on special days such as the day of your conversion.

Think of the sacrificial love a mother has for her baby. She goes through excruciating pain for the birth of her baby and sacrifices her time, and sometimes her occupation, for her baby. I have the same kind of love for you. Think of the sacrifices I gave up, My home in heaven because of My sacrificial love for you. I endured pain and suffering on the cross for you. I even made the ultimate sacrifice—giving My life—so that you might be forgiven. When you remember the sacrifices I have made, you can begin to comprehend My unselfish love. *Pray: Lord, I know Your passionate heart for the lost.*

Parents have children whom they love with all their heart. There is nothing they would not do for them; and if you watch them walking through a toy store, you would think there is nothing they would not buy for them. They want their children to have everything they need and want, within boundaries. Then I your heavenly Father want to do everything I can for My children. The Bible says, "Your Father knows what you need before you ask him" (Matt. 6:8 NIV).

Because I your heavenly Father love you wholeheartedly, I give you the privilege of prayer. I invite you, "Ask, and it will be given to you; seek, and you will find; knock, and it will be opened to you" (Matt. 7:7).

Wholehearted love is wonderful. I want you to wholeheartedly love Me, because I first loved you wholeheartedly. *Pray: Lord, I revel in Your wholehearted love for me.*

In response, I want your wholehearted dedication to Me. Just as an Old Testament believer had to sacrifice a whole lamb to Me in worship, so I want you to sacrifice your whole heart, body, and soul to Me. Paul says, "I beg you to sacrifice your whole self to God because He has been so merciful to you" (Rom. 12:1 ELT).

Next, I want you to serve Me wholeheartedly with your time, talents, and treasures. Again, Paul said, "And whatever you do, do it heartily, as to the Lord and not to men" (Col. 3:23).

Finally, you must praise and worship Me wholeheartedly. When you bow in worship, there must be nothing between your soul and Me.

YOUR TIME TO PRAY

Lord, I come into Your presence to worship You wholeheartedly;
I give You everything I have—everything;
I give all my money (treasure) to Your control,
I will spend it only as You direct me.
I give You all of my time,
I will use my time only as You direct me.
I give You all of my talents to accomplish Your will;
I will do whatever You direct.
Take my praise and be glorified in the worship I bring.
Amen.

38

I HAVE A NOSE—THE SENSE OF SMELL

> *And the LORD was pleased with the aroma of the sacrifice and said to himself, "I will never again curse the ground because of the human race, even though everything they think or imagine is bent toward evil from childhood. I will never again destroy all living things."* —Genesis 8:21 NLT

What is the sweetest smell in the world? To some women it may be perfume. To some men, it may be the grease from a motor they are tuning up. To a mother it might be talcum powder on her baby. What is the sweetest smelling aroma you have ever smelled? A barbeque steak? Hot donuts? An incense candle?

To Elmer Towns, one of the best smells was breakfast by a Northern Canadian lake. He was president of Winnipeg Bible College and two friends took him fishing in the summer of 1964.

They drove north 100 miles on a paved road, and then he felt the gears shift down as they ran out of pavement and traveled another fifty miles on a sandy road. Then they took off cross-country on a deer trail to an Indian village. There he met their guide, an 81-year-old Indian whose grandfather had been chief of his tribe. The elderly guide asked Elmer, "Would you like to meet my father?"

Elmer was already surprised at the guide's age, so he was intrigued to meet his dad, a 101-year-old man, bent with age. His skin was shriveled from too many cold winters. The man's father advised me, "Eat what my son cooks...you can live as long as I have."

Towns and his friends left the Indian reservation and arrived at an abandoned gold mine after dark. As you can image, there were no convenience stores or snack shops in the Canadian north woods. So, although hungry, he crawled into a sleeping bag and immediately went to sleep.

Elmer felt his sleeping bag shake before dawn the next morning. Quietly the 81-year-old Indian nodded for him to get dressed and follow him to a bank overlooking the lake. The old Indian had started a tiny fire, so tiny that its solitary flame looked too small to cook anything. Three burning sticks produced a small shaft of smoke curling straight up though the pine trees. There was not a trace of breeze anywhere. An old-fashioned galvanized coffee pot was percolating coffee in the fire over the three sticks.

Without saying a word, the Indian poured a cup of bubbling hot coffee. Towns smelled the coffee before taking a sip.

The smell was so delicious Elmer's eyes watered. It was too hot to drink but the aroma was irresistible. He blew into the cup and then sipped it. Still too hot.

So, Elmer sat down to embrace the smell.

He had enjoyed many other delectable smells, but that early morning, the guide and the remote setting miles from civilization enhanced his favorite smell...fresh brewed coffee.

What about Me your God? What was the most irresistible smell to ever enter My nostrils? Maybe the extremity of Noah's sacrifice and the setting made the smell of roasting meat irresistible to Me. Noah had lived in the ark for over a year. Not once did Noah have a chance to offer a burnt sacrifice to Me in that boat. Did Noah have fire for cooking on the ark? Did Noah think a burnt sacrifice might have caught the ark on fire? The first thing when Noah planted his sea legs on *terra firma* was to seek fellowship with Me his God.

Noah and his sons gathered stones. There a huge pile of brushwood on top of the logs. They killed an animal before laying its meat on the wood on the altar. The fire was kindled, and animals sacrificed to Me, the God of the flood and the God who saved them.

I was pleased when I saw Noah and his sons making Me their priority. Noah's family did not selfishly hold back any animals, thinking, "We do not have many left." No, after I had safely delivered them from the storm and flood, they wanted to say thank you to Me, their Savior. Their sacrifice said to Me, "We desperately need fellowship with You."

Animal offerings in the Old Testament had many purposes. Some offerings were for transgressions, some for unknown sins, some for worship, and some for nothing more than communion with Me, their Lord and God. Noah's burnt offering represented all of the above.

"The LORD smelled a sweet savour..." (Gen. 8:21 KJV), and was pleased. Noah was not bringing a sacrifice out of habit. Noah brought a sacrifice because of his relationship with Me. Noah brought a sacrifice because he walked with Me.

What did I like about the smell? My enjoyment of the smell was not a selfish thing, like much of your own. Humans selfishly enjoy the smell of a pie baking. You lie on the lawn to enjoy the smell of freshly mown grass, or the smell of fresh clean sheets on a bed invites you to sleep.

I smelled the results of Noah's devotion and obedience—and was pleased. What have you offered to Me, your Lord and God that would smell sweet to My nose? *Pray: Lord, I offer to You my instant obedience.*

I want to forgive the sins of everyone because I love the world. I never delight in punishing anyone. When Noah approached Me through a blood offering, I the God of the universe was pleased with Noah's obedience when I smelled the smoke of roasted meat on the fire.

Several times in the Old Testament I pointed out that idols of clay or metal "neither see, nor hear, nor eat, nor smell" (Deut. 4:28). Dumb idols do not have the function of people. Idols cannot do anything I can do, so I the Eternal Person enjoyed pointing out their limitation. Idols cannot see, nor can they hear the petition of followers. An idol cannot even smell the roasted smell of sacrifices offered to it.

When Israel chose to bring sacrifices to Me (see Lev. 1–7), on each occasion I was pleased with the smell of the burning sacrifice. I looked beyond what I smelled, and looked beyond what I saw on the fire. I looked into the hearts of those who offered the sacrifice and was pleased. *Pray: Lord, be pleased with my body as a sacrifice to You.*

YOUR TIME TO PRAY

Lord, You were pleased with the sacrifice of Noah
When he presented a burnt offering to You.
Be pleased when I offer my body to You (see Romans 12:1-2).
Lord, You want me to give everything I have to You;
I surrender all of my self and possessions to You.
Be pleased with what I sacrifice to You.
Amen.

39

I HAVE EYES

> *For the eyes of the Lord are on the righteous, and His ears are open to their prayers....* —1 Peter 3:12

The church was packed on Mother's Day, so all the families could not sit together. The mother sat with the youngest child in front of father who was attempting to hold young John, a hyperactive and playful child.

The whole church sang a familiar hymn, "This is my Father's world, and to His listening ears...." Little John had learned a comic song in kindergarten that involved putting his hands behind his ears and waving them.

"*John*, put your hands down," Mother said from her seat without looking around. She knew what her son was doing.

Later during the sermon, little John stood behind his mother; no one noticed he was standing because he was so short. He examined his mother's hair carefully without touching it. He looked at it from the left...right...and bottom. Finally, he parted her hair, at which she turned around and made him sit down.

At home, mother asked in exasperation what he was doing with her hair. "I was looking for your eyes in the back of your head." Because

Mother had caught him doing so many things when she wasn't looking, little John heard she had eyes in the back of her head.

Did you know I the Lord God have eyes?

I do, but they are not in the back of My head. In fact, I do not have literal eyes. The "eyes of the Lord" is a metaphor to help you understand My personhood. You need eyes to see things so you can know them. I know all things but without the necessity of physical eyes.

My knowing is called *omniscience*. I know all things—past, present, and future—both actual and potential. I know all things without effort; I do not have to strain to remember as you do. I never forget. *Pray: Lord, You know everything about me. You know all my needs. I worship Your vast knowledge.*

I know all things because I am *omnipresent*, equally present everywhere all the time. Since I am everywhere, I know everything, everywhere, at that same time. *Pray: Lord, You know all the good things I do, and the times I disobey. Forgive me, cleanse me, and restore me.*

I even know things about people that you cannot know. You cannot know people's thoughts. You may know their actions, but you do not know what your friends are thinking. But I know. "O Lord, you...know everything about me. ...you know my every thought. ...You know what I am going to say before I even say it" (Ps. 139:1-2,4 TLB).

Yes, I have eyes to know you, but My eyes are a metaphor. I do not have blue eyes or brown eyes—I have all-knowing eyes. Because My eyes see all you do, the verse at the beginning of this chapter says I am open to hear your prayers. I know if you are sincere, and I know if you are honestly trying to keep My commandments. *Pray: Lord, see my sincere effort and hear my prayers.*

What do My eyes see? I see your actions, your thoughts, your dreams, your good, and your sin. I the Lord see the evil in people's hearts. "The face of the Lord is against those who do evil..." (Ps. 34:16). That ought to be a warning to all. The fact that I have eyes to see ought to influence you when you pray. No one is without sin, but in the integrity of your heart, you like Paul can have "a conscience, void of offense to Me" (Acts 24:16 ELT). *Pray: Lord, forgive my sin that You see in me. Also, see the integrity of my heart.*

My ability to see goes beyond My believers. I the Lord see everything in every person. "For the eyes of the Lord run to and fro throughout the whole earth..." (2 Chron. 16:9). There's no place where people can hide from Me, their Lord. My eyes see everything. "I can never get away from my God! ...even darkness cannot hide from God..." (Ps. 139:7,12 TLB). *Pray: Lord, shine Your face on my life, forgive my sins and keep me from evil.*

Also, do not count on Me missing your sins because I am sleeping. I see everything, all the time, in every place. I never sleep. "He will never let me stumble, slip or fall. For He is always watching, never sleeping" (Ps. 121:4 TLB).

YOUR TIME TO PRAY

Lord, I take comfort in Your all-seeing eyes.
You see and know all I do and think;
Forgive me when I slip or commit a presumptuous sin.
Cleanse my heart from hypocrisy.
Lord, because you see all I do,
I come to You with a humble heart,
Asking for mercy and forgiveness.
Hear my heart's prayers, and give me the prayers
That are asked within Your will.
Amen.

40

I HAVE WAX IN MY EARS

> *I am the LORD who has an arm that is not too short so I cannot save you, and My ear is not plugged up with wax so I cannot hear you, but your sins have created a barrier between Me and you and your iniquities have stopped up My ears, so I will not hear.* —Isaiah 59:1-2 ELT

I your Lord and God am all powerful. I can do anything I want to do, I am everywhere present at the same time, and I know everything there is to know, both actual and potential. But "I cannot hear your prayers. Why? Look at this verse, "...your iniquities have separated between you and your God" (Isa. 59:2 KJV).

Why don't I listen to your prayers, and why do I not even begin to answer them? It is not My inability; it is My nature that is holy. I am so holy and pure that I cannot look on sin without judging it. That means I cannot hear iniquity without judging it. So, I will not hear when you are living in sin, and I will not answer when your prayers are motivated by sin.

I do actually hear your prayers that are corrupted by sin, or your prayers that are motivated by sin. Because I know all things. But as James says, "Sometimes you ask and don't get what you request because you ask...to satisfy your lust" (James 4:3 BBJ). Because I know sin, I reject prayers that arise from the lust of your heart.

In fact, My ears were plugged with wax...that's right, wax. The father's sins were like earwax that blocked My hearing. Isaiah 59:1 in the King James Version says that My ear is "heavy." The Hebrew word for "heavy" is the same word used for "blockage." Wax is an external residue that builds up in the ear canal to block sound from reaching the eardrum.

Do I hear? Yes, I have the ability to hear communication from the human voice. I hear everything you say, and I know everything you think. When it is said, I have earwax and cannot hear you; it means your sins (earwax) are a blockage between you and Me.

If I can hear, then does that mean I have ears? No! I do not have ears, eyes, or a mouth. I am Spirit nature and I do not have physical organs. When you say "God's ear" that is an anthromorphism—your projections of human organs onto Me so you can understand how I do things. Though I am Spirit without a physical body or human organs, I still possess the abilities or functions these organs provide.

I want to hear your prayers. Remember I said, "Ask, and it will be given to you; seek, and you will find; knock, and it will be opened to you" (Matt. 7:7). Asking is the rule of My Kingdom. It is My way of keeping My people close to Me.

Don't try to hide things from Me. "I, your Lord, have searched you and I know your thoughts...before your tongue speaks a word, I, your Lord, know what you are going to say" (Ps. 139:1,4 ELT).

So how do you express your prayers so I will give attention to them? And beyond My acknowledging your request, how can you pray and get answers? First, begin with the model prayer My Son Jesus taught you, "Hallowed be Your name..." (Matt. 6:9). You recognize My holiness. Even before you recognize your sinfulness, look to My purity. Your attitude is more important than the words you pray, for I see the heart: "I search people's hearts and I know what they think..." (Jer. 17:10 BBJ).

Only when you see My holiness will you properly see and understand your sinfulness. Sin is not your weakness or lack of education or any human stumbling, sin is rebellion against Me. When you ignore My authority and break My commands, it is the same as telling Me "no" to My face. I judge sin.

When you pray to Me, come asking forgiveness by the blood of My Son. He said, "Your sins are forgiven through the shedding of My blood" (Eph. 1:7 BBJ). You do that when you obey Jesus. "Whatever you pray, asking in My name, I will do it, so that My Father will be glorified in Me" (John 14:13 BBJ).

This is praying in faith—knowing Jesus will answer your request, even before you ask. So what is faith? Jesus said, "You can't please My Father without faith, so come to Him because you know He exists and you know My Father will reward those who earnestly seek Him" (Heb. 11:6 BBJ).

All that I have said about getting your prayers answered deals with your relationship to Jesus and Me. But sometimes My children ask and don't get what they request. Remember, I have a plan and purpose for My work in the world.

"...If we ask anything according to His will, He hears us" (1 John 5:14). This verse directs you to ask or pray according to My will, or My plan. I don't hear and answer requests that are contrary to My purpose.

James expresses another truth about prayer: "You do not have what you pray for because you don't ask rightly" (James 4:3 BBJ).

Sometimes you ask for requests that may take time to deliver the answer. You don't plant seeds one day and pray for fruit from the plant the next day. I work through My laws of nature. Seeds need time to grow roots, then a bud, next leaves and stems...finally fruit. So, when you pray in faith for answers, but the results are not automatic or quickly realized.

Remember, I am the energy of the laws of nature, I take time to develop your answer through My laws of growth. So, "Keep on asking and you will receive. Keep on seeking and you will find. Keep on knocking, and the door will open" (Luke 11:9 BBJ).

Blocked prayers make you examine yourself. Why are your prayers not getting through? I use earwax to get the attention of My followers—or any sinning believer—or you. Examine yourself in light of My standards. *Pray: Lord, show me any sin in my life so I can effectively pray.*

The next time you have trouble hearing something or you need to have your ears cleaned out, think of My ears. Maybe I am having trouble hearing everything you pray because you are responsible for the earwax that is blocking your communication with Me. *Pray: Lord, forgive my sin and hear my prayers.*

YOUR TIME TO PRAY

Lord, I now realize my prayers are not answered
Because there is sin in my life
That blocks my prayers from reaching You.
Lord, show me any hidden or ignorant sin that blocks
My prayers from reaching You.
I confess to You that I am a sinner;
Forgive me and hear my prayers.
Amen.

41

I USE MY FINGERS

> *"This is the finger of God!"* the magicians exclaimed to Pharaoh.... —Exodus 8:19 NLT
>
> *When I look at the night sky and see the work of your fingers— the moon and the stars you set in place.* —Psalm 8:3 NLT
>
> *When the LORD finished speaking with Moses on Mount Sinai, he gave him the two stone tablets inscribed with the terms of the covenant, written by the finger of God.* —Exodus 31:18 NLT
>
> *They were trying to trap him into saying something they could use against him, but Jesus stooped down and wrote in the dust with his finger.* —John 8:6 NLT

The phrase "finger of God" was first used by the Egyptian magicians to describe the plague of gnats that infested their whole land. The Egyptian magicians used the word "finger" eloquently and expressively to describe a curse on the people of their land. In the previous miracle of frogs, God punished the Egyptians so that "They [frogs] will come up out of the river and into your palace, even into your bedroom and onto your bed! They will even jump into your ovens and your kneading bowls. Frogs will jump on you..." (Exod. 8:3-5 NLT). "But the magicians were able to do the same thing with their magic. They, too, caused frogs to come up..." (Exod. 8:7 NLT).

But the next miracle-plague was swarming gnats or lice covering the Egyptians and their animals. "Pharaoh's magicians tried to do the same thing...but this time they failed" (Exod. 8:18). The magicians then announced the gnats plague was the "finger of God" (Exod. 8:19). This phrase, like "the hand of God," was used to communicate power or judgment, but specifically God's divine authority or evidence of God's desire.

Later Moses wrote in Exodus that the Ten Commandments were written by the finger of God. If God only spoke and Moses wrote down the Ten Commandments, that suggested Divine Source, but for God to actually write down the Ten Commandments with His finger, that carries double authority. God not only was the Source of the laws expressed in the Ten Commandments, God gave it His personal endorsement of power or authority. Since the Ten Commandments were written by the finger of God, that added the idea that every word was imperative, or to express it in modern times, every word was God-inspired and inerrant.

To the ancient Asians, the finger expressed more authority than what the mouth could say. In other words, it was important for a person to put it into writing, rather than just speaking the idea. This is illustrated by the power of military commands or orders.

As a result, the Asian world decorate the finger with precious metals such as gold and silver, plus expressions and ostentatious gems. After speaking, they waved the hand and fingers as an authoritative display of power—riches were considered equal with legal power.

When the psalmist used the finger of God to describe the creation of heaven, this was a glimpse of the enormous power of God. If the night sky, moon, and stars are a picture of the enormous power of God's finger, compare that to the brilliant power of the total sun.

The finger of God denotes power and authority as seen in God writing the first copy of the Ten Commandments. "When the Lord finished speaking with Moses on Mount Sinai, he gave him the two stone tablets inscribed with the terms of the covenant, written by the finger of God" (Exod. 31:18 NLT)

Also, Jesus said, "If I cast out demons with the finger of God, surely the kingdom of God has come upon you" (Luke 11:20). Again, Jesus' finger was symbolic of the power of healing. "A deaf man with a speech impediment was brought to him.... Jesus led him away from the crowd.... He put his fingers into the man's ears. Then, spitting on his own fingers, he touched the man's tongue" (Mark 7:32-33 NLT). The man was healed.

Finally, think of the occasions God instructed the priests to use their fingers when applying blood in the act of sacrificing animals to God (Exod. 29:12,20; Lev. 4:6; 9:9; 14:14,16-17).

When the Pharisees brought the woman caught in adultery to Jesus they wanted to argue the points of the law. The life of the woman apparently meant nothing to them, the law meant everything. They asked Jesus, "The law of Moses says to stone her. What do you say" (John 8:5 NLT). The fact Jesus used His finger twice to write on the ground tells us by pictures that He understood the significance of the "finger" in determining the power and force of divine law. His use of the finger pictures God's power with the Pharisees.

Obviously, God the Father and the Holy Spirit do not have fingers. Jesus described His heavenly Father as, "God is Spirit (John 4:24). But also, just as obvious, Jesus had fingers and on one occasion used it to write on the ground. So to speak of the finger of God, we look at the power a finger represents, and we also see God is able to do the things a finger would do. A finger is an anthromorphism. Yet when we come to Jesus, He had a body that was planned for Him before He was born (1 Peter 1:19-20). Also planned for Him for eternity past (Heb. 10:4). Therefore, could it be said that the second Person of the Godhead actually wrote the first giving of the Ten Commandments in stone?

YOUR TIME TO PRAY

I never realized how important a finger was until I lost its use.
For a week my index finer (pointer) was bandaged because of a cut.
I could not write, throw a ball very hard, or get things,
Out of my right pocket without dropping it.
Then I realized my finger does what my mind thinks,
As it accomplishes in life what I desire or choose.
Lord, You get everything done that You think, and You
Accomplish everything You want—without fingers.
Thank You for knowing I need fingers to work,
And get done the things in life I need to do.
Thank You for creating Adam with fingers, and through generations,
I have fingers, and a mind to make fingers work for You.
May my fingers do Your work and please You.
Amen.

Section D

LEARNING MY DIVINE NATURE

God is who He is, and you can reach out to study Him to get a limited understanding of Him. Only God understands Himself perfectly. The nature of God is His essence (this Section D). This section discusses God's being and without it He would not be God.

42 – I Am Intelligent Designer

43 – I Am God of Law

44 – I Am Unknown, the God of Mystery

45 – I Am Spirit

46 – I Am Invisible

47 – I Never Change

42

I AM INTELLIGENT DESIGNER

> *I have revealed Myself from heaven to all...truth about Me that is obviously seen in nature and the universe...all can see clearly My power and intelligent design in everything I have created, so they have no excuse of rejecting Me.*
> —Romans 1:18-20 ELT

Suppose there were nothing in the world but bricks. Suppose these bricks were shown to you in two different pictures. Suppose the first picture is a huge pile of bricks. The second picture is the same amount of bricks perfectly designed into a brick wall that has patterns of beauty and order, yet extremely useful.

The first pile of bricks doesn't tell you anything about the origin of the bricks. Where the bricks came from, who made them, etc. When you examine the bricks, they are all the same size and composition. You conclude, somewhere there is a "brick maker" who had an original purpose to make bricks. The pile of bricks is enormous, so tall, you cannot see the top of the bricks, and so wide you cannot see around them. So, you conclude the brick maker is extremely big and powerful. Since all the bricks arrived at one time, you conclude the brick maker made a one-time decision to make bricks.

These bricks illustrate the universe is made up of a pile of atoms. The atoms are not limitless, only I the Creator God am limitless. But there are more atoms than humans can count. Everything you discover from atoms tells you there is an atom-maker who decided to make atoms, and who has enormous power to make an enormous number of atoms—bricks.

Now look at the brick wall. You first noticed the design in the brick wall. You assume at least three things from the unique and beautiful brick wall. First, the maker of the brick wall had a blueprint or pattern or design to guide his assembling of bricks into the wall. Second, the maker of the brick wall had the power or ability to construct the bricks into the design that was suggested to him in his blueprint. Third, the maker of the brick wall had the craftsmanship, talent, and ability to construct and fashion the wall into its finished condition.

"The heavens reveal the enormous power that God used to create such a vast universe, the sun, moon and planets display His craftsmanship. Day after day continually show the design God built into creation, and night after night they tell of His ability and power" (Ps. 19:1-2 ELT).

The designing images of the universe reveals an Intelligent Designer, and the vast greatness of the universe suggest a powerful Creator. The universe has order and a useful design implying it was put into place by an Intelligent Creator who knew what to do and where to place each part, all suggesting a functioning universe.

Psalm 94:9 reminds us that I am the One who "planted the ear" and "formed the eye." I put them there for a purpose. It is obvious there is a Designer when you view the laws of nature that continually guide, replenish, and make the earth useful. This is also seen in the law of human and animal reproduction, as well as reproduction of plants and all things that grow. There is an intelligent plan within the Creation—My purpose, which is both powerful and driven by design.

UNDERSTANDING THE PERSON OF GOD

My infinite power as Creator alone is not enough to demonstrate that I am a Person or that I am a Personal Being. An enormously large universe does not prove I am Person only that I have enormous powers. But when the element of purposeful design is added, this leads to the conclusions that I am an Intelligent Creator—Brick Maker who directed Myself to continually make bricks and recreate My creations.

When all bricks or atoms are the same, this only suggests I the Creator only made a choice to make bricks in one way, in one size, from the same components. But when I the Brick Maker used the power of intelligent choice to place the bricks in a design that is purposeful and beautiful, that suggests I am the Intelligent Designer.

But I the Creator-Brick Wall Maker, add another component of your understanding of Me. I have the ability to understand and create order and beauty. As a result, I created a design of bricks in the wall I created that had purpose and usefulness. I the Creator-Brick Wall Maker used My mind to produce the desired effect. But remember, I also have the power to create and control, to place bricks in a wall according to My design and purpose. The evidence of design in the universe leads to the conclusion I am a Designer, an Intelligent Designer. The size, scope, and craftsmanship of the universe leads to the conclusion that I a Person began it all.

YOUR TIME TO PRAY

Lord, You are powerful, more powerful than
Anything in the universe You created.
I bow to Your plans and want Your influence.
You are Jehovah, "I am that I am," the self-directing Lord.
Just as You choose to create the world for a purpose,
Help me find Your purpose for my life.
Designer, You placed Your nature and purpose into the universe,
Help me understand Your purpose for all things.
Help me understand and accomplish Your design for my life.
Amen.

43

I AM THE GOD OF LAW

> *I love God's law with all my heart.*
> —Paul, Romans 7:22 NLT

All laws—whether natural law, mathematical law, or any law that governs the function of the universe or the human body—are expressions of My nature and My purpose for humankind and the universe. All people are subject to My purpose and control at all times—laws of nature, laws controlling your physical body, civil jurisprudence, business laws, spiritual laws, and moral laws.

Some have defined law as a "rule of action," others describe it as the standards for life, or an expression of common goodness for all. Others describe law by its consequences when its rules are not observed.

Law is not something that I the God of the universe conceived and delivered to My followers as I gave the Ten Commandments (implied laws) to Israel (Exodus 20). All law is an extension of My nature and person and is the power or force by which I carry out My purpose in the universe. The law is not like Me, nor does law describe or define Me. No, law is Me. Law is an extension of My nature and Person. It is My power and energy by which I run and rule the universe.

Law was not something created for humans. Law always existed—like Me the God of the universe, for I have always existed, and law has always existed. Law is My nature.

Law allows for human independence from Me, yet at the same time humans remain dependent on Me. A human is described as an independent-dependent person, independent of Me (I am not a human and a human is not Me), yet at the same time all humans are dependent upon Me.

Everything I create is the offspring of who I am and bears the impression of My determinate nature. Because man was made in My image, humans have My nature with certain limitations and modifications. I created man an intelligent being. Man was not made in My exact image, but after My likeness (Gen. 2:7). As such, man was created as an independent being with freedom and opportunity. Yet man's freedom introduced a moral dilemma into My economy. How could man be independent yet accountable to Me his Creator? How could I the omnipotent God control My universe, yet allow freedom in My creatures? The answer is in law.

All of My created beings are unalterably related by law to Me their Creator. And by law people relate one to another and by law they live and survive and prosper in this universe. By law they relate to Me their Creator. There was no other way for Me to create a moral being who would be free, yet accountable to Me his Creator.

THE NATURE OF LAW COMPARED TO MY NATURE

1. The law of God is an expression of Me and is an extension of My nature. Therefore, the law and My nature are similar to the sun and its rays. Just as rays are an extension of the sun and deliver the life and energy of the sun to all it touches, so law extends My decisions and makes standards and My energy to all I create. I understand all I do, and My law extends Me and My purpose to all. Also, I am the Source of all wisdom and knowledge, and from Me comes the eternal understanding of My laws. The source of the law is My nature. Therefore, the law reflects My wisdom and understanding of Me.

2. **The law is an extension of truth, which is a reflection of My nature.** Truth is what is consistent with itself and corresponds to nature. Law is an extension of My nature and communicates the veracity of My being. The law must be truth, for it is an exact representation of My nature and must be consistent in its application to all. My law is consistent in punishments of the disobedient, and consistent in rewarding the obedient.

3. **The law is a unity, because I am unity.** This means the law is always consistent with Me and with itself. It never differs from one individual to another—it is universal in its application and it is perpetual in its obligation. Every person is obligated to Me, through the law of God. That means everyone is accountable to Me, their Creator—that includes everyone—the law reaches to all.

My whole system of law involving humankind and creation is symmetrically magnificent. There are no anomalies in My plan. Every law or principle is constitutionally adjusted and adapted to every other principle or law and fits perfectly into one giant unifying plan over which I am the supreme governing, sustaining, sovereign Head. Humans are part of that system, being created by Me, fitting into My unifying plan and answerable to Me.

4. **The law is eternal as I am eternal.** Since I am without beginning and ending, then My law is applicable to every being, every situation, and every relationship in all places for all eternity.

5. **The law is immutable because I am unchangeable.** Because the law is an extension of My nature, it is as immutable as My divine nature. It could

not change unless My nature can change. The idea of change with reference to Me would destroy My perfection, and therefore destroy My existence.

I cannot repeal My law, nor can I give another system of law different from the present law without contradicting My own nature. As a result, if I repealed My law, I would destroy Myself. But I "who cannot lie" affirms the law and every relationship it touches. The law prescribes duty for all of its subjects; hence everyone must obey the law.

THE LAW IS A REFLECTION OF MY MORAL ATTRIBUTES

Every quality including the law comes from My nature, which is the source of all things. But the law also objectifies My attributes. Since attributes radiate from My nature to magnify My Person, then each of those perfections logically requires the other; and combined together they form My infinite majesty. To understand My moral law, you must see it in symmetrical relationship to My attributes. The law for My creatures is a moral law and of necessity is a picture of My moral nature.

1. The law is holy. Since I am holy, it follows that My law must be holy. This means it must not require anything contradictory to My nature. The law and its obedience must be in conformity to My holiness who created it.

2. The law must be just. As such, law must be an extension of My impartiality. Justice is the negative side of My positive holiness. The law must treat all beings equally, demanding conformity by every person. Nonconformity to the law will bring consequences—punishment. Obedience will produce happiness. My attributes and law are a symmetrical embodiment of My infinite nature; holiness without spot, justice without partiality, and infinite goodness without compromise.

3. **The law is also the embodiment of My benevolence and kindness.** Where the law is followed, it elevates humans—My created human beings—to the level of My expectation. The person who keeps My law is good and is happy. Therefore, obedience to the law leads to happiness. I am love, and I love My creatures.

THE RELATIONSHIP OF THE LAW BREAKER TO ME

I, the Lord God, created man; therefore, all people have an obligation to Me for their existence. On the other hand, I am responsible for My creatures; I must be humanity's benefactor. Since My whole system—including the laws governing the universe, humans, and angels—is a unity, not one of My laws can be changed, and not one offense can be condoned.

How can I save the system when there is rebellion? I must punish the rebel, and everything affected by the rebellion. My system must be restored and balanced. Again, it is impossible for the law to pardon the rebel or to accept rebellion.

Rebellious people must suffer the penalty of each law they break. However, this does not mean that pardon is not available. Someone outside the system must enter and provide pardon. But first, that person must compensate the system and satisfy the demands of the law.

If law could pardon, then law would destroy itself, for it would render itself null and void. For law to pardon an offense is to say that laws existence is not essential. Even I the Lord God who is the essence of law, cannot pardon the lawbreaker, because then I would encourage a rebellion to My law—I would be in conflict with Myself. My law is inexorable and unbending. My demands of the law must be satisfied. My holiness, justice, and goodness make the law unpardoning.

The gospel does not superintend a new law into the legal system. Nor does the gospel make a "milder law" by which I can extend My pardon to humankind. Man was placed under a law that required perfect obedience. Without perfect obedience, there was automatic punishment.

Also, I the Lord God cannot pardon by mere prerogative. Just because I the Lord God desire to pardon the sinner does not mean that I would forgive the sin. I the Lord God can create worlds, and I can make man in My image, but I have no prerogative to change My own nature.

HUMANS: INDEPENDENT-DEPENDENT PERSONS

My laws are the centripetal forces that constantly draw a person into constant relationship with Me. *Centripetal* literally means to seek the center as the centripetal force draws the planets to the sun. *Centrifugal* literally means to fly from the center as forces that revolve around the sun tend to fly away from the sun. The centrifugal forces describe the autonomous and independent natures of humans. These two forces created man as an independent-dependent person. He was drawn to Me, yet at the same time he is pulled away from Me.

Humanity is obligated to My spiritual law. Because both man and law are extensions of My nature, there is a reciprocal relationship between humans and the laws which govern them. Human personality, reflective of My nature, independence, constitutes the centrifugal force that drives people into an independent orbit away from Me. Humankind is dependent upon Me. My compelling love is the centripetal force that draws people back into harmony with Me. Both forces were properly equalized before the Fall.

The Bible describes My voice walking in the garden in the cool of the day—humanity and I in fellowship. The original human nature was properly adjusted to the place of My orbit; human nature reflected My nature and character. Humans are independent people. That is because man was created in My image. But at the Fall, man's independence allowed him to rebel away from the center of his life, which was Me. To this day, humans are not aware of their rebellion against Me; modern men and women feel they are only following their individuality. Yet they are lost in sin and need My salvation.

You do not know what would have happened if man (Adam) had continued his life, living in harmony with My laws. You would assume that the race would have multiplied, every individual would have lived in harmony with reverence for other individuals. You can only assume that all of civilization would have lived in harmony with the physical world. But sin—rebellion to Me—changed everything.

Both Adam and Eve rejected Me and followed their independent drive while rejecting their dependent obligation to Me. "When Adam sinned, sin entered the world. Adam's sin brought death, so death spread to everyone, for everyone sinned" (Rom. 5:12 NLT).

Because I am holy, I must judge the sin of Adam and all who are born in sin and commit sin. Yet at the same time, I am love, and I have infinite love for Adam and all other persons born in the human race.

I sent My Son Jesus Christ to be born as a human, but He was born without sin (2 Cor. 5:21; Heb. 4:15; 1 Peter 2:22; 1 John 3:5). He was born under the law and perfectly kept the law. On the Day of Atonement when the Jews offered a perfect lamb for the forgiveness of the sins of the nation (John 1:29), I allowed Jesus to die on a cross for the sins of the world (John 3:16). His sanctified the demands of the law becoming the substitute who died for the sins of all.

I Am the God of Law

YOUR TIME TO PRAY

*Lord, forgive me for my blindness to You and Your law.
I thought I was following my free will to find happiness,
But then I realized my freedom was my rebellion against You.
Thank You for Your law that revealed my sinful acts,
And then Your law showed me my sinful nature.
Lord, Your law condemned me but didn't save me.
Then Your gospel told me that Jesus was sent
Into this world to live a perfect life without sin.
Your Son was without sin, yet in death He became my sin.
I accept Your perfect love in sending Jesus to earth,
And the perfect love of Jesus who died for my sins.
The cross is the great conqueror of my sin—all sin.
Your offer of enteral life is overwhelming.
How can I do other than give You my entire life,
And serve You with all my strength for all my days.
Amen.*

44

I AM UNKNOWN— THE GOD OF MYSTERY

> *Abraham planted a tree in Beersheba and called there on the name of the unknown Lord, El Olam, the God of mystery.* —Genesis 21:33 ELT
>
> *The LORD our God has secrets known to no one. We are not accountable for them, but we and our children are accountable forever for all that he has revealed to us....* —Deuteronomy 29:29 NLT
>
> *God...has made known to me the mystery...that was kept secret in past ages...that the Gentiles are fellow-heirs, members of the same body...in Christ Jesus.* —Ephesians 3:3-6 ELT

In ages past I had a secret, a mystery, that Old Testament believers did not understand. They were born Jews, members of the nation of Israel. At the time, I directed My promises to Abraham and his seed. I worked primarily with the Jews, although I was not limited to them only—Rachel, Ruth, etc. That secret was revealed through Paul to the world that Christ Jesus died for the world. Now all believers—Jews and Gentiles—were one body in Christ.

I Am Unknown—the God of Mystery

When I call Myself mystery, what does that word mean? First, a mystery is that which is kept secret or not explained. It is not that people could not understand the truth of the mystery, it was withheld from them. It had to do with timing. A mystery was left unexplained until a later time. That is what Paul refers to in Ephesians 3:1-12. This mystery was "hidden in God" (Eph. 3:9) until "it might be made known" (Eph. 3:10).

The second meaning of mystery is that which cannot be known. There are mysteries in the universe that science cannot explain, facts that puzzle them. It accepts certain facts or trust, although the power or principle that caused it cannot be explained. Gravity, for example, is a sample of a mystery that is not understood. Gravity is a force or attraction that pulls all things to the center of the earth. Scientists don't know where gravity came from, what is the source of its power, why it is perpetual, or why they cannot alter it or turn it off. Believers know I am the Source of law, including gravity. I use gravity to hold all things in place. Gravity is a mystery; you must take it by faith, just as you must accept My existence by faith.

The third meaning of mystery is puzzling or inscrutable, or in essence, unknowable. Certain things that I do you will never understand because you are human, and I am Deity. "'For My thoughts are not your thoughts, and neither are your ways My ways,' says the LORD" (Isa. 55:8). Isaiah goes on to say, "For as the heavens are higher than the earth" (Isa. 55:9), he means, "My reasons for doing things are higher than your reasons."

My title *El Olam*, God of mystery, was first revealed at the desert oasis Beersheba, at the well that Abraham had dug. It was the last well from which a traveler could get water before entering the desolate Sinai Peninsula, making Beersheba strategically located. This well had been taken from Abraham violently by the servants of Abimelech, the tribal chieftain of the Philistines.

Abraham reproved Abimelech, and out of this confrontation came a covenant of peace. The agreement between Abraham and Abimelech was certified by animal sacrifice and accompanied by an oath. Abraham also "planted a grove in Beersheba and there called on the name *El Olam*, the God of mystery (Gen. 21:33).

Scholars have attempted to determine why My name *El Olam* was revealed at this particular time and place. Some have suggested that this is the place where Abraham first exercised faith to claim the Promised Land, giving Abraham and his descendants the land of Palestine as part of the "everlasting *(olam)* covenant" that I made with Abraham (Gen. 17:7). There is mystery or hiddenness *(alam)* here. It is a mystery why I the Lord God chose that land for Israel.

Since the future was hidden *(alam)* from Abraham, he called on Me who mysteriously know the future ages. As the apostle Paul teaches, these Old Testament events were shadows or types of what was to come in Christ. For example, the birth of Isaac of a "free woman" and Abraham's rejections of the "son of the bondmaid" is a picture of My dealing with the Jews and later with the Gentiles (see Galatians 4:22-30). Since these things are done in mystery—their fulfillment awaits a dispensation *(olam)* yet to be revealed—they are in My hands, *El Olam*, the God of secrets and mysteries.

YOUR TIME TO PRAY

I believe what I read in the Bible and I
Try to understand everything You say and do.
But sometimes I don't understand all I read,
So, like Abraham, I trust You when
I cannot see the future.
You are trustworthy, for I understand and know
I believe because You said so in Scriptures,
And I have seen Your promises fulfilled in my life.
I don't know everything about You, El Olam,
Sometimes You are mysterious and unknown.
But I trust You because I have seen Your goodness in action.
I have felt Your protection, and You have guided me.
I accept Your love to me in Christ's death
For the forgiveness of my sins.
I love all I know of You.
I trust You even in things I don't know.
Amen.

45

I AM SPIRIT

> *I am Spirit, and those who worship Me must worship in spirit and truth.* —John 4:24 ELT

Throughout the Bible, I am called *Spirit*. Though corrected in the New King James Version, the original King James Version wrongly added "a" when it translated this verse, "God is a spirit" (John 4:24 KJV). It was suggesting I have a spirit. In fact, I do not have a spirit; I am spirit in nature. But I am not like a spirit as the world defines—the spirit of capitalism, the spirit of St. Louis or a ghost that some call a spirit. No! I am spirit in nature. I am original Spirit before creation when all other spirit(s) come into existence.

When you say I am spirit, you are saying I am immaterial and invisible. When the religions of the world make an idol, they are limiting their god to what they can get their hands on. But I told you, *"You shall not make for yourself a carved image—any likeness of anything that is in heaven above, or that is in the earth beneath, or that is in the water under the earth; you shall not bow down to them nor serve them"* (Exod. 20:4-5).

Although My spirit nature is immaterial and invisible, I am said to have hands (see Isa. 65:2), feet (see Ps. 18:9), eyes (see 1 Kings 8:29), and fingers (see Exod. 8:29). But these are not to be understood as My actual physical parts. They are anthropomorphisms, whereby you project physical characteristics on Me to help you understand that I do the functions of these physical parts.

To understand Me as spirit is also to realize I am omnipresent, or present everywhere at the same time. This not only means My spirit nature can be in every geographic location simultaneously, but also in every time--past, present, and future--all at once.

There are times in the Bible when people said they saw Me (see Gen. 32:20), or they saw a manifestation of Me (see Exod. 3:6; 29:9-10; Isa. 6:1). In fact, they didn't actually see Me; they saw the reflection or *spirit* of Me. They saw the results of Me, but they didn't actually see Me directly. I was in the pillar that led Israel through the wilderness, and they saw the cloud of fire that hid Me, but they didn't see Me (see Deut. 4:15). "No man has seen God at any time" (John 1:18).

Individuals saw Me physically for the first time when they saw Me in the flesh. When they saw Jesus of Nazareth, they saw God in the flesh. "No one has seen God at any time" (John 1:18), John wrote to reinforce this truth, and later declared, "I myself have seen Him with my own eyes and listen to Him speak. I have touched Him with my own hands. He is God's messenger of life" (1 John 1:1 ELT).

As Paul wrote, "When the fullness of time had come, God sent forth His Son" (Gal. 4:4). Even though you can't see Me now in the flesh, you can see Me in the pages of Scripture. You can know how I was born... how I lived...what miracles I did...and how I died for you. Your heart can know Me experientially, as if you were to touch Me with your fingers. *Pray: Lord, You live within me and You give me spiritual energy to live for the Father, Son, and Holy Spirit.*

YOUR TIME TO PRAY

Lord, You are spirit without physical form,
Yet I see You in my heart when I pray.
I trace Your image in the pages of Scripture.
You are everywhere present in Your universe.
I hear Your voice in the wind,
And I see your fingerprint in the Blue Ridge Mountains.
Lord, You manifest Yourself in the Scriptures
And when I can't see You with my physical eyes,
Then I see You in my heart.
Amen.

46

I AM INVISIBLE

> *Christ is the image of the invisible God.*
> —Colossians 1:15 ELT
>
> *...He is the eternal King, the unseen one....*
> —1 Timothy 1:17 NLT
>
> *It was by faith that Moses.... He kept right on going because he kept his eyes on the one who is invisible.*
> —Hebrews 11:27 NLT

"Why can't I see God?" the little boy asked his father.

The father thought a moment, then answered, "Because there is nothing to see."

The boy's father was half right and half wrong. The father was right in that I don't have a physical existence, so I cannot be seen. The father was wrong when he said, "There is nothing to see." I have existence, but I cannot be seen. I your Lord and God am not physical; yes, I don't have a body. The Bible declares, "God is Spirit" (John 4:24), but I am real—a real spirit with life, energy, and personality. I am a Person—I think, I have feelings, and I can make decisions. I can choose what I want to do, or what I want to happen in My universe. I may be an eternal Spirit, but I have always existed. I am real.

UNDERSTANDING THE PERSON OF GOD

Back in eternity past, We the Trinity planned the creation of the universe, and a human who would live on planet Earth. We created the first man, Adam, in Our image and likeness. We knew Adam would sin because We are timeless. We live in the past, present, and future at the same time. So, We planned salvation for fallen Adam and any human creations who expressed saving faith.

I the Father sent My Son to become human to live among humanity without sin. My Son Jesus said to Me, "You did not want animal sacrifices and sin offerings, but you have given me a body to offer" (Heb. 10:5 NLT). I am the invisible God, but My Son was born a baby to the virgin Mary. In that birth He was given a human body. It was in that body He died for the sins of the world. Jesus rose again in that body to demonstrate victory over death, sin, and satan. He is now seated at My right hand in glory in that body (Acts 2:34). One day Jesus will return to earth in that body to judge all sinners and punish satan in hell. Yes, Jesus has a body, but the Father and the Holy Spirit are invisible.

There are many reasons why you cannot see Me. Heathen bow down to an idol they can see, and the limits of that idol tell them the limits of their god and their faith. I am not limited to a body; I am limitless; I am bigger than the universe.

When you realize the trillion of light years to cross the universe—I am not only bigger than the universe, I live beyond the outer limits of the universe. There you launch out into the nothingness beyond space. I am there without limits; I am limitless and eternal. That is only one reason why you cannot see Me.

But I am invisible. I am around you above you and in you (Ps. 139:7-12). I know your thoughts before you say them (Ps. 139:4). I was living in you when you originally thought of a word to say. Then later when you spoke what you thought, I was there to hear you. I am beyond time, beyond space, beyond your thoughts of Me. I am limitless. I am God!

Because of what I am, I must be invisible—for you cannot comprehend all of who I am, and all of what I do.

YOUR TIME TO PRAY

Lord, I pray to You because You are here, even when I cannot see You.
I learn of Your existence in the Word of God, even when You cannot be seen.
I listen to You speak to my conscience and guide me,
Even when my outward ears do not hear.
I feel Your intimate presence when I worship You,
Even when You cannot be seen with the eye.
I know You are real, for You live in my heart...
You give me joy...assurance...and hope in the future.
You may be invisible, but that doesn't mean You are not real, or You are not alive.
Even though I cannot see You with my eyes or touch You with my physical hands.
You are as real as I am alive.
And You live in me, and I live in You.
Amen.

47

I NEVER CHANGE

For I am the LORD, I do not change. —Malachi 3:6

People change constantly. They change their minds, change their views, and change their preferences. Their bodies, knowledge, and hairstyles all change. But I never change. My nature is ultimate perfection in all I am, say, and do, and it never has or will change. Therefore, I am perfect. I never change nor have I gotten better over time nor will I get better in the future.

The same can be said for My getting worse than I am. I am not an old man who loses his strength, his ability to concentrate, or his ability to do things. I am embodied perfection since the beginning of time, and I have not changed.

My unchanging nature is often called My immutability: "For I am the Lord, I do not change" (Mal. 3:6). How do you know I am immutable? The Bible provides a number of examples of My steadfastness.

I am unchanging in My existence. Psalm 90:2 (NIV) proclaims, "Before the mountains were born or you brought forth the whole world, from everlasting to everlasting you are God." I have always been and always will be in existence (see Deut. 32:39-40; Ps. 9:7; 55:60; 102:12; Hab. 1:12; 1 Tim. 1:17; 6:16). *Pray: Lord, I trust You because You've always been here for me and You always will be.*

I Never Change

I am unchanging in My justice. Zephaniah 3:5 reads, "The LORD is righteous...He will do no unrighteousness. Every morning He brings His justice to light; He never fails...." Since My nature demands that I judge sin and I am immutable, I can't change My mind about punishing those sinners who reject My Son. *Pray: Lord, I thank You that Jesus died for my sins and forgave me.*

Thankfully, I am also unchanging in My mercy (see Deut. 7:9; 1 Chron. 16:34). Psalm 106:1 reads, "Praise the LORD! Oh, give thanks to the LORD for He is good! For His mercy endures forever." Though My justice is fixed, My mercy has no limit. It never runs out, never runs dry, and covers all of your sins. *Pray: Thank You for Your unending mercy and forgiveness.*

I am unchanging in My holiness: "I am the LORD your God; consecrate yourselves and be holy, because I am holy..." (Lev. 11:44 NIV). The word "holy" means to be set apart. From beginning to end, I have been set apart, pure, and unblemished. *Pray: Lord, I praise Your unending holiness.*

I am unchanging in My truth and My knowledge. In the Psalms, David calls out "Redeem me, O LORD God of truth" (Ps. 31:5 ELT) and writes "For the LORD is good; His mercy is everlasting, and His truth endures to all generations" (Ps. 100:5). Later in chapter 139, David praises Me for My knowledge: "Before a word is on my tongue you, Lord, know it completely. ...all the days ordained for me were written in your book before one of them came to be" (Ps. 139:4,16 NIV). *Pray: Lord, thank You that Your truth is everlasting and that You know me inside and out.*

In addition to My immutable nature, My love and promises are also unchanging. Not only do I love My people so much that I sent My Son to die for your sins (see John 3:16), I have always loved you (see Ps. 107:1) and will always love you. I not only love you; I love everyone who is not saved and has not turned to Me. I want all of them saved (see 2 Pet. 3:9). *Pray: Thank You for loving me eternally.*

In the same way, you can have confidence in My unchanging promises: "Know therefore that the LORD your God is God; he is the faithful God, keeping his covenant of love to a thousand generations of those who love him and keep his commandments" (Deut. 7:9 NIV). Since My promises are immutable, you can rest in My pledge to you (see Rom. 4:21). *Pray: Lord, thank You for the strength of Your promises.*

"Immutability" is another word to describe My unchanging nature. You can have confidence in the immutability of My existence, justice, mercy, holiness, truth, knowledge, love, and promises to you. When things around you seem to change from day to day or you buckle under the pressures of the world, you can stand firm in your faith knowing that I am steadfast.

YOUR TIME TO PRAY

Lord, I thank You for Your unchangeableness.
You've been the same throughout my life.
I thank You for Your love and goodness to me;
You have given me much more than I deserve.
Lord, I worship You as my rock and my strength,
When I change, You change not.
When I sin and confess my iniquity to You,
You forgive me as You promised to do.
Amen.

Section E

LEARNING MY ABSOLUTE ATTRIBUTES

THE ABSOLUTE ATTRIBUTES OF GOD

- I am all-powerful – Omnipotent
- I am all-knowing – Omniscient
- I am everywhere present at the same time – Omnipresent

The key to understanding a description of Me is seen in My attributes. The absolute attributes of omniscience, omnipresence, and omnipotence refer to the ability or power of My person, and are true only about Me. Humans do not have these unlimited abilities—they possess the presence and a limited understanding of these attributes.

> 48 – I Am All-Powerful – Omnipotent
>
> 49 – I Am All-Knowing – Omniscient
>
> 50 – I Am Everywhere All the Time – Omnipresent

48

I AM ALL-POWERFUL—OMNIPOTENT

> *For with God nothing shall be impossible.* —Luke 1:37 KJV
> *...with God all things are possible.* —Matthew 19:26

I can do everything that I want to do; nothing is impossible for Me. I created this vast and powerful universe just by speaking what it was to become. But that's only a small aspect of what I have power to do. I am omnipotent, meaning I have all power, greater than anything you have ever seen, or could ever imagine.

The speed of My planets traveling through space is amazing. The burning intensity of the fiery stars is majestic. Their size is mind-boggling to humans. The sun is over one million times larger than our small earth where you live. In the next galaxy is Antares, which is 64 million times greater than your sun. In another galaxy is Hercules, which is 110 million times the size of Antares. Finally, there is Epsilon, several million times larger than any other star. *Pray: Lord, You are infinite, without limitations and all powerful. I bow in awe to worship You.*

This vast universe is beyond your comprehension, yet the creation of just one man was so much greater. When you consider your smallness in comparison to the universe, you cry out with the psalmist, "When I look at the night sky and see the work of your fingers—the moon and the stars you set in place—what are mere mortals that you should think of them, human beings that you should care for them?" (Ps. 8:3-4 NLT).

My power is seen in the small, intricate things that you humans can observe but could never achieve on your own. I can imbed DNA in every molecule, and I poured My mighty power into an atom of protons, neutrons, and electrons, with the electrons swirling around the nucleus with awesome nuclear force.

I can raise the dead, walk on water, count the hairs on your head, and all the hairs of all the heads of the seven billion souls on the earth. I do all this without effort. What I decide, is carried out (see Isa. 59:1-2).

You can see and understand My power. I didn't withhold it nor did I hide it: "For since the creation of the world His invisible attributes are clearly seen, being understood by the things that are made, even His eternal power and Godhead, so that they are without excuse" (Rom. 1:20).

My power holds everything together: "He was before all else began and it is his power that holds everything together" (Col. 1:17 TLB). When you see the almost limitless power of a nuclear explosion when the atom is split, it forces you to ask, "What holds all the trillion times trillion times trillions of atoms together?" The answer? My power!

There are things I can't do. I can't do impossible or absurd things, such as make $2 + 2 = 3$. Also, I can't do things that are contrary to My nature, such as create sin.

UNDERSTANDING THE PERSON OF GOD

THINGS I CAN'T DO

- I can't make a square circle.
- I can't make yesterday not happen.
- I can't see a thing that's not there.
- I can't deny My existence (see 2 Tim. 2:13).
- I can't lie (see Heb. 6:18).
- I can't be tempted to sin (see James 1:13).

I can do whatever I will to do, but I do not necessarily will to do everything. I could have exercised My power to keep sin out of the world, but that would have been inconsistent with My will to allow people created in Our image to exercise their free will. Since you are created in the image of Me who has free will, I allow you to exercise your free will. Why? Because I want honest worship.

Remember, authentic worship and fellowship is only authentic when praise flows freely from one who chooses to magnify Me. If you talked like those baby dolls with recording devices to say only what it was manufactured to say, then your praise would mean little to Me. *Pray: Lord, I choose to love You and worship You. Thank You for creating me free—free to worship.*

When Eve ate the fruit and sinned, I could have destroyed satan and evil, but I allowed sin and satan to exist. So, in your continued testing, you demonstrate your love to Me by choosing to obey Me. Therefore, My all-powerful nature is controlled by the purpose of My will for you. *Pray: Lord, I will find Your will for my life and do it.*

Because I reign over My universe, My power makes everything accomplish My perfect will. So, I am sovereign over things seen and unseen, over the material world and the unseen spiritual world. But most of all, I have power over you because you were made in My image. For those who believe in Me, ask for forgiveness and obey Me, for I have the power to "work all things for good" (Rom. 8:28).

YOUR TIME TO PRAY

Lord, I am awed by Your power and majesty,
Beyond anything I can comprehend.
I worship You and praise You
For I am fearfully and wonderfully made.
Lord, You can do everything You desire.
Be merciful and gracious to me;
I am Your servant.
Amen.

49

I AM ALL-KNOWING—OMNISCIENT

> *I am great and have great power. My understanding is infinite.* —Psalm 147:5 ELT
>
> *To the only wise God....* —Jude 1:25 KJV

You may strive to know about Me, or to know Me intimately, but your knowledge pales in comparison to the knowledge I have of you. I know all things, past, present, and future, and understand all things from the most complex scientific processes to the innermost thoughts of your soul.

Since I am eternal, I was present when everything was created, so I have knowledge of all things since the beginning. I have never had to learn anything. Also, since I am not limited to time, I exist in the past, the present, and the future. Therefore, I can't forget anything since I was living when everything happened in the past. I have all knowledge.

Since I am omnipresent, meaning I am present everywhere at the same time, I know all things because everything happens or exists within My presence, no matter where or when they occur.

The word "infinite" means without limits. Since I am infinite, I am not limited by space, time, power, or knowledge. I know and understand the sum total of all knowledge and wisdom. I even know those things humankind has yet to discover. Nothing surprises Me.

Since I am wise, I know the potential of everything that might have happened but didn't occur. The Bible says I "calleth those things which be not as though they were" (Rom. 4:17 KJV), which suggests I am wise enough to know what would have happened to you, if you took an alternative of every decision you've ever faced.

When Elmer Towns was going through Bible college, he checked out all the girls on campus for a potential wife. As men are apt to do, they usually chose the ones they thought were good-looking, smart, and had a great personality. Elmer chose Ruth Forbes, who in his opinion was the best looking, smartest, and, thankfully, the most spiritual of all the girls in his freshmen class.

God knows what would have happened to Elmer if he had married any one of those other girls.

When Elmer thinks of being married to someone other than Ruth, he shutters with fear to think of the mistake he might have made. Continually he praises Me for his choice in choosing Ruth. I am wise and good. *Pray: Lord, thank You for every good decision You've led me to make.*

It is important to realize that I have not learned all these things. If you say that I learned, you would be saying that I did not know something in the past and that would make Me imperfect and less than God. But this is not the case. Instead, I know everything before it happens to you and before you learn it. The prophet Isaiah asks, "Who has directed the Spirit of the LORD, or as His counselor has taught Him? With whom did He take counsel, and who instructed Him, and taught Him in the path of justice? Who taught Him knowledge, and showed Him the way of understanding?" (Isa. 40:13-14). The answer? No one! Therefore, I have never had to learn anything.

I also know all things equally well. Some people know a few things about a lot of different topics. Other people have a great amount of in-depth knowledge about a specific area, but My knowledge and understanding is infinite in everything and in every way: "...all things are open and exposed, and revealed to the eyes of Him" (Heb. 4:13 AMP).

Consider this one area: There are trillions and trillions of stars, and every day it seems scientists are finding new stars and galaxies never before seen or known to mankind. But the scientists are wrong in saying new stars are being created; it's just that they are finding those stars that already exist. In the Psalms, David recounts, "He counts the number of the stars; He calls them all by name. Great is our Lord, and mighty in power; His understanding is infinite" (Ps. 147:4-5). I already know the exact number of stars and have a name for each. *Pray: Lord, I trust Your future for me.*

And that's only a small glimpse of My infinite knowledge! Whatever an infinite mind knows, only an infinite mind understands, for only an unlimited mind has unlimited understanding. Because you are limited, you can never fully know Me, but what you do know about Me, should cause you to worship Me for My greatness. *Pray: Lord, I worship You for Your greatness and majesty.*

Finally, since I know everything, you can have confidence that I have a plan for your life. "I know the plans I have for you," says the Lord, "They are plans for good and not for evil, to give you a future and a hope" (Jer. 29:11 TLB). Since I know you and know your future, wouldn't you like for Me to lead you today? Wouldn't you like Me to show you My will for your life? *Pray: Lord, I wait for Your leading.*

When you talk about My omniscience, you mean I possess perfect knowledge of all things. The prefix "omni" means "all" and the word "science" comes from a Latin root meaning "knowledge." My omniscience has all knowledge in this world and in eternity. My knowledge is infinite, which means without limits of time, space, or topic. I know all things, from the solutions to the world's most complex problems to the quiet ponderings of your heart.

YOUR TIME TO PRAY

Lord, I praise You for Your infinite wisdom and knowledge.
Lead me in this life to do Your will.
I know You have a good plan for my life;
Give me joy as I follow Your leading.
I need Your wisdom and direction. Guide me in all decisions.
Amen.

50

I AM EVERYWHERE, ALL THE TIME— OMNIPRESENT

> *You can never get away from My presence. If you could go to heaven, I am there; if you make your bed in hell, I am there. If you could fly away on the wings of a new day, and fly across the sea, even there you would find My hand guiding you.* —Psalm 139:7-10 BBJ

The theologians have said I am present everywhere at the same time. They called this My *omnipresence*. The prefix "omni" means "all," so I am present at all places. The word "presence" means "in front of you." So, I am here and everywhere else at the same time.

My omnipresence demonstrates My immensity. In other words, since I am present everywhere at the same time, I am big--really big. I exist in every place at every time. In Psalms David writes, "I can't get away from God, He's everywhere" (Ps. 139:7 ELT). Even when you travel to the last star and jump off into blackness of nothingness, I am in the blackness of nothing.

I am also infinite, without limits or boundaries. Do I have a center? Technically, My center is everywhere. Even David said, "Where can I flee from Your presence?" (Ps. 139:7). The answer, of course, is nowhere.

But what happened after Cain killed Abel? The Bible says, "Cain went out from the presence of the Lord" (Gen. 4:16)? How did Cain leave Me if I am everywhere? The truth is that Cain couldn't get away from My presence; Cain only left the place of My blessing and usefulness. Cain left his relationship with Me.

There are several ways to describe My presence. First, there is My *localized presence* where I make My presence known in an actual, physical location. I was present in the Shekinah glory cloud that covered the tabernacle of meeting when I led the Israelites through the wilderness (see Exod. 40:34-38). When I spoke from heaven at the baptism of Jesus, I said, "This is My beloved Son in whom I am well pleased" (Matt. 3:17), which also demonstrated My localized presence. I localized Myself to help you understand My ministry to you and to focus your worship on Me.

Second, My presence can also be an *indwelling presence*. When you are saved, I come to dwell in your heart. Galatians 2:20 (NIV) says, "I have been crucified with Christ and I no longer live, but Christ lives in me." God the Father can also indwell you (see John 14:23) as well as the Holy Spirit (see John 14:17). As a child of God, it's comforting to know God lives in you. *Lord, help me be a good testimony, I will carry Your presence wherever I go.*

Third, I can manifest Myself in an *institutional presence*. Just as I dwelt in the Holy of Holies in the Tabernacle, My Son Jesus comes to live in His institution, the Church (see Matt. 16:18). Jesus promised, "where two or three are gathered together in My name, I am there in the midst of them" (Matt. 18:20).

Sometimes Elmer Towns walks into a church meeting and can feel My presence. I your God am working in hearts and My *institutional presence* in the church motivates him to preach the Word with boldness.

Then too, Elmer Towns has been invited to preach in churches that are cold and dead. He does not feel My presence in their services. Those churches need a spiritual revival.

Revival comes when I bring My presence to My people. In Peter's sermon in Acts, I promised, "I will pour out my Spirit in those days" (Acts 2:18). Sometimes you can actually feel Me pouring Myself on a group of people as they sing. How do you know it is My presence and not just stirred up emotions or mass hysteria? Because I promised to come and sit on the throne in the middle of people praising Me. "...I am holy, enthroned in the praises of Israel" (Ps. 22:3 BBJ). What you are experiencing is a small taste of revival. *Pray: Lord, pour out Your Spirit on Your people—pour Yourself on me.*

Finally, there is My *omnipresence*, which means I am present everywhere at the same time. This omnipresence means that I see all and know all. Hagar wisely said, "You are the God who sees me" (Gen. 16:13 NLT).

So, am I in the tavern where people are getting drunk? Yes, so don't do it in My presence. Am I in the bedroom where a couple is committing adultery? Yes, so don't do it in My presence. Am I present where every sin is committed, where every lie is told and wherever My name is blasphemed or used as a curse word? *Pray: Lord, when You see things in my life that displease You, forgive me.*

I Am Everywhere, All the Time—Omnipresent

YOUR TIME TO PRAY

*Lord, I know You are present everywhere today.
I know You are in my life;
Today, let me feel Your presence.
Lord, You are already present everywhere I am going,
So protect me there.
Be with me in every encounter in my life today.
Thank You for Your love and protection.
Wrap Yourself around me wherever I go today.
I know You have a great plan for my life;
Guide me to do Your perfect will always.
Amen.*

Section F

LEARNING MY MORAL ATTRIBUTES

THE MORAL ATTRIBUTES OF GOD

- I am Love
- I am Holy
- I am Good

My moral attributes describe things that are also true to a much lesser extent in people. These attributes include holiness, love, and goodness. While Christians should have a holy lifestyle, love others, and do good deeds, these three attributes exist in their pure form only in Me.

I am described as "holy" in the Scriptures (Ps. 111:9; Isa. 57:15). Because I am holy, you also should live holy lives (Lev. 19:2). I am also described by the statement, "God is love" (1 John 4:8,16). Your responsibility to love one another as a Christian is tied to My demonstration of love in saving you (1 John 4:11). Also, Jesus noted, "No one is good but

One, that is, God" (Mark 10:18). Because I am good, I have worked in the lives of Christians to equip them to do good works.

> 51 – I Am Love
>
> 52 – I Am Holy
>
> 53 – I Am Good

51

I AM LOVE

> *For God so loved the world that He gave His only begotten Son, that whoever believes in Him should not perish but have everlasting life.* —John 3:16

Love is perhaps My most popular attribute. When children are asked to describe Me, they eventually say "love." But love is not just what I show to a person, or the compassion I express for a person; I am the Source of love. I am love. "He who does not love does not know God, for God is love. ...And we have known and believed the love that God has for us. God is love, and he who abides in love abides in God, and God in Him" (1 John 4:8,16).

To say I am love makes Christianity unique among the religions of the world. Many of the gods of the heathen religions are angry; some are even hateful beings. Those who worship idols think their god punishes them, and they blame their god for every bad thing that happens to them. That's why the heathen gods need constant appeasing.

But I the God of Christianity am different. I do not do bad things to people, but I tell you in the Bible why bad things happen. I remind you that you live in a fallen world where germs and bacteria spread disease, where hateful people do hateful things, where accidents harm you, where things break down, where rust and weeds eventually take over, and when your aging body weaken you, you finally die. You were born into this world with no knowledge so you must learn everything you need to know to protect yourself, advance yourself, and provide for your life, liberty, and pursuit of happiness.

You also live in a world in which people die. A little boy, standing behind the right shoulder of his dad who was driving the family station wagon, asked, "Does everyone have to die?"

"Yes," the father wistfully answered.

"Even if they get lucky?" the little boy chirped.

"Yes," was all that the father could say.

Death is an enigma that chokes the life out of every person. You know you will die. It is a pressing question that you must face. In fact, this question was asked in the oldest book written in the Bible: "If a man dies, shall he live again?" (Job 14:14).

I had to punish Adam and Eve because of their disobedience in the garden. If you were in the eternal theatre watching the events in the Garden of Eden unfold before your eyes, you might have asked, "Will God kill them?" Didn't I promise death if they disobeyed Me, saying, "In the day you eat, you shall die"?

Look at My final act in the theatre of salvation. I didn't kill them, but someone had to die. My Son Jesus stepped away from My throne to say, "I'll go to earth to die in their place." Jesus didn't just die for Adam and Eve, He said, "I'll die for all mankind."

You might ask from your theatre seat, "Why would Jesus do that, and why would the Father let Him do that?"

"Because of love," I would answer you.

"What is love?" you ask.

"Love is giving yourself to the one you love."

The love of My Son Jesus is described as a relationship to a friend: "Greater love has no one than this, than to lay down one's life for his friends" (John 15:13). When you try to find the greatest expression of love, it's when you give yourself for others.

Later John said, "Here is where you understand the love of God for you: it's when Jesus laid down His life for you" (1 John 3:16 ELT).

Then finally John said, "Here is love...God loved you and sent His Son to satisfy the debt you owe to Him" (1 John 4:10 ELT).

The greatest declaration of love is John 3:16: "For God so loved the world that He gave His only begotten Son, that whoever believes in Him should not perish but have everlasting life."

It may be possible for some people to give possessions, money, or time without loving the person to whom they give, but it's impossible to totally love without giving yourself totally.

JOHN 3:16—THE **GREATEST** VERSE IN THE BIBLE

For God—Greatest *being*

So—Greatest *degree*

Loved—Greatest *affection*

The World—Greatest *object of love*

That He gave—Greatest *act*

His only—Greatest *treasure*

Begotten—Greatest *relationship*

Son—Greatest *gift*

That whoever—Greatest *company*

> Believes—Greatest *trust*
> In Him—Greatest *object of faith*
> Should not perish—Greatest *deliverance*
> But have—Greatest *assurance*
> Everlasting—Greatest *promise*
> Life—Greatest *blessing*

Love is the opposite of selfishness. As a matter of fact, love is perfect unselfishness. Love gives itself completely to the one it loves. Look how a mother does everything for her baby.

Only the strong can love because they must have strength to reach out of themselves to another. They do that in spite of what they want or need. I am the Source of all strength; I can give Myself to you because I am the Source of all love. I can give Myself and never empty Myself. I can never come to the end of My love. Why? I am perfect love, the Source of love and the total expression of love. I am "the God of love" (2 Cor. 13:11) and have all "the love of God" (2 Cor. 13:14). *Pray: Lord I bathe in Your love.*

In the King James Version, the love chapter of the Bible, 1 Corinthians 13, translates the word "love" as *charity*, such as: "Charity suffereth long, and is kind; charity envieth not; charity vaunteth not itself, is not puffed up...Charity never faileth" (1 Cor. 13:4,8 KJV). Some modern readers criticize the Bible for using the out-of-date term charity for love. Yet when you look at why charity is used, you get a deeper meaning of love. Charity meant giving time and money to a worthy cause, such as a church, the Red Cross, or some other nonprofit charity. Therefore, those who originally wrote the King James Bible saw love as giving oneself to those who were thought worthy. That's love. *Pray: Lord, teach me ultimate giving.*

But My love is far greater: "For scarcely for a righteous man will one die; yet perhaps for a good man someone would even dare to die. But

God demonstrates His own love toward us, in that while we were still sinners, Christ died for us" (Rom. 5:7-8). *Pray: Lord, I say thank You.*

YOUR TIME TO PRAY

Lord, Thank You for Your constant love to me;
Even when I sinned, You loved me.
You always forgive me and love me.
Thank You for looking after me in love,
Even when I forgot to think of You.
You always love me and protect me.
Lord, Thank You for Your constant love and
Continuing grace;
You love me, forgive me, and guide me;
I'm in Your constant loving care.
Amen.

52

I AM HOLY

> ...the High and Lofty One who inhabits eternity, whose name is Holy.... —Isaiah 57:15
>
> ..."You shall be holy, for I the LORD God am holy." —Leviticus 19:2

The first description of Me that usually comes to your mind is I am love. The second is most likely, I am holy. Maybe it's because you sing, "Holy, holy, holy..." offering praise to Me for My holiness. But do you know what you mean when you call Me holy?

Holiness means "to separate" or "to cut off." To be holy means to be separate from anything that is evil. It has a dual meaning: to be separate from sin and to be separated out for My use. Stop and ask yourself, *Am I holy?* If you are honest, you will answer no. "If we claim to be without sin, we deceive ourselves and the truth is not in us" (1 John 1:8 NIV). If you think you are perfect or good enough to go to heaven, you don't know My standard. "There is none righteous, no, not one" (Rom. 3:10).

What about committing just one sin? What if you just slip once in a while? "If we claim we have not sinned, we are calling God a liar..." (1 John 1:10 NLT).

So what's your answer to your sin? When you become a Christian, I forgive all your sins (see John 1:29), and I also declare that you are perfect or righteous in My Father's sight. This means you are justified in My presence in heaven: "Being justified by faith, we have peace with God, through our Lord Jesus Christ" (Rom. 5:1). Some have tried to explain justification with the phrase: "Just as if I've never sinned."

When My Son Jesus took your sin on the cross, He gave you His perfection. So now you have positive holiness. You have the record of Jesus' perfect life transferred to your account (see 2 Cor. 5:21).

What do you mean when you pray the Lord's Prayer and say, "Hallowed be Your name...on earth as it is in heaven" (Matt. 6:9-10)? The word "hallowed" means holy, so you are praying for My holiness to rule on this earth, just as it rules heaven. But this earth is a big place, so you should focus your prayer on the place you live. "Holy be Your name in my life where I'm living on earth today." *Pray: Lord, be holy in my life today.*

My holiness is both active and passive. It is passive in that I am already holy without doing or saying anything holy. I am holy because I am perfect in all I am and do, and My holiness is the perfection of My moral nature. The angels in heaven cry, "Holy, holy, holy, Lord God Almighty, who was and is, and is to come!" (Rev. 4:8).

I am also actively holy. Everything I do is holy, meaning My actions are without sin. I cannot lie (see Titus 1:2) and I always speak the truth (see John 17:17). I cannot be tempted with sin (see James 1:13), and holiness is the primary motivation of all I do.

I did not make Myself holy because if I did that, then holiness is something I decided to do. It means I was not holy at one time, and I became something different from what I was. But I cannot change. I am eternal, and I have always been holy.

You may have a difficult time understanding the nature of holiness. It's something the human mind struggles to understand. A.W. Tozer suggests, "We cannot grasp the true meaning of divine holiness...it stands apart, unique, unapproachable, incomprehensible, and unattainable. The natural man is blind to it."[1] *Pray: Lord, what I cannot understand, teach me.*

So, what can you do? David said, "If I regard iniquity in my heart, the Lord will not hear [me]" (Ps. 66:18). So, you must confess any sin in your life (see 1 John 1:9), and constantly walk in fellowship with My Son Jesus Christ. For the Bible says, "If we walk in the light, as He is in the light... the blood of Jesus Christ His Son cleanses us from all sin" (1 John 1:7). Then you must constantly keep yourself from any future sin (see 1 Cor. 11:30-32).

I am too holy to look on sin. That's why I turned My back on My Son Jesus when He was on the cross. The cross is where My Son Jesus became sin for you. Therefore, My Son Jesus cried out, "My God, My God, why have You forsaken Me?" (Matt. 27:46). *Pray: Lord, thank You for becoming my sin.*

YOUR TIME TO PRAY

Lord, I cry "Holy, holy, holy" because You are holy.
I worship in Your holy presence,
Knowing You are pure and without sin.
Lord, Forgive my sin by the blood of Jesus Christ
Who gave His life to die for me.
I confess my sin and repent of every known sin,
Clothe me in the righteousness of Jesus Christ.
Lord, I will worship You in Your perfection and holiness,
Accept my praise that I bring in the name of Jesus.
Amen.

NOTE

1. Elmer Towns, *Theology for Today* (Ft. Worth, TX: Harcourt and Brace, 1999), 112, #34.

53

I AM GOOD

> *So Jesus said to him, "Why do you call Me good? No one is good but One, that is, God."* —Luke 18:19

Cameron, 4-year-old great-grandson of Elmer Towns, volunteered to pray the blessing when the family went out for a Sunday meal at a local restaurant. Every Sunday, Elmer invited any of his daughters, ten grandchildren, and three great-grandchildren who were able to attend. He wanted to create positive memories among his family members. Sometimes it cost Elmer almost $300, but the rewards are priceless. So one Sunday, Cameron prayed in a loud voice for all to hear:

> God is great
> God is good,
> Let us thank Him for our food,
> By His hand
> We all are fed,
> Let us thank Him for our daily bread.
> Amen.

After the prayer Elmer congratulated him on doing a great job, and asked, "Do you really think God is good?"

Cameron answered, "He's given me this meal, hasn't He?"

Great wisdom from a little mind! And immediately Elmer forgot all his theology—he thought he had paid for the Sunday meal.

In a broad sense, My goodness includes all the positive things I do and have done for you when I do it directly or through another source.

When the rich, young ruler came to question Jesus about salvation, he asked, "Good Teacher, what shall I do to inherit eternal life?" (Luke 18:18). Isn't it an interesting fact that a rich man was worried about his inheritance after this life? Jesus answered him, "Why do you call Me good? No one is good but One, that is, God" (Luke 18:19).

Yes, I am good. I am not an angry God, such as found in heathen religions. I am good in My nature, and I do good things to all people I created, specifically to My unique children.

Moses told Israel, "He [God] will do thee good" (Deut. 30:5 KJV). I am God who created the world and "saw that it was good" (Gen. 1:25). As a good God I said, "It is not good that man should dwell alone" (Gen. 2:18), so I created Eve. My Son Jesus calls Himself, "the good shepherd" (John 10:11). Jesus said some were, "good seed" (Matt. 13:24), and He said to the Pharisees, "Many good works I have shown you" (John 10:32).

My goodness is seen in many of My attributes and, in a greater sense, these are part of My goodness. One of these attributes, My *mercy*, represents My goodness to those in distress or misery.

When David sinned with Bathsheba, I convicted David so greatly he thought he would go to hell (see Ps. 51). David prayed, "Have mercy upon me, according to Your lovingkindness; according to the multitude of Your tender mercies, blot out my transgressions" (Ps. 51:1).

The tax collector prayed fervently in the Temple, and, "would not so much as raise as his eyes to heaven, but beat his breast saying, 'God be merciful to me a sinner!'" (Luke 18:13).

Mercy flows from Me because I am its Source. "The mercy of the LORD is from everlasting to everlasting on those who fear Him..." (Ps. 103:17).

Mercy is available to a whole range of individuals. The Bible speaks of My mercy to My church (see 2 Cor. 1:3), to believers (see Heb. 4:16), to Israel (see Isa. 54:7), and My mercy to those who are called (see Rom. 9:15,18). My mercy provides truth to you that I am indeed good.

My *grace* is another expression of My goodness. I expressed My grace to the ill-deserving and to those who deserve My punishment. My grace is the opposite of My justice. In grace, I give to people the exact opposite of what they deserve.

They deserve condemnation, but I give them salvation.

They deserve hell, but I give them heaven.

They deserve death, but I give them life.

They deserve alienation, but I give them Myself.

Grace also is unmerited favor. There was nothing in you that deserved My goodness: "Even when we were dead in trespasses, [God] made us alive together with Christ (by grace you have been saved)" (Eph. 2:5).

In My goodness I acted in grace to save you: "The grace of God that brings salvation hath appeared to all men" (Titus 2:11). Paul wrote "For by grace you have been saved through faith..." (Eph. 2:8).

In response to My grace you should be thankful and live for Me: "By the grace of God I am what I am, and His grace toward me was not in vain, but I labored more abundantly than they all, yet not I, but the grace of God which was with me" (1 Cor. 15:10). You should grow stronger in grace because My goodness has been shown to you: "But grow in grace, and in the knowledge of our Lord and Savior Jesus Christ..." (2 Pet. 3:18). *Pray: Lord, I say I am grateful, help me mean it.*

A third attribute of Mine is My goodness as seen in My benevolent supply I give for the welfare of mankind. Jesus tells you My benevolence extends to all people: "He makes His sun rise on the evil and the good, and sends rain on the just and the unjust" (Matt. 5:45).

Paul used My good, benevolent nature as a reason why people should get saved: "He did good, gave us rain from heaven and fruitful seasons, filling our hearts with food and gladness" (Acts 14:17).

Finally, My goodness is seen in My longsuffering, or patience. I should have destroyed mankind because of Adam's sin, but I didn't. I am good in that I wait for people to repent and turn to Me (see Rom. 2:4). "The LORD is...slow to anger and great in mercy" (Ps. 145:8).

My longsuffering is the patience whereby My love and goodness overshadow My holiness and judgment: "The Lord...is longsuffering toward us, not willing that any should perish, but that all should come to repentance" (2 Pet. 3:9).

What should be your response to My goodness? Because I am good, and because I have given you the goodness of salvation, you should "hold fast what is good" (1 Thess. 5:21). You should do "good works" (Matt. 5:16) and "Depart from evil, and do good" (Ps. 37:27). *Pray: Lord, I will do ministry for You, make it good.*

YOUR TIME TO PRAY

Lord, You are good and merciful to me;
Thank You for Your grace and kindness in saving me.
Help me live a godly life of holiness,
And be a testimony of Your grace.
Lord, You are good, gracious, merciful, and kind,
I worship You for Your longsuffering of me.
Help me live righteously for You.
Amen.

Section G

LEARNING MY DIVINE NAMES

The study of Me—the doctrine of God—includes a study of My names because they reveal My nature and work. In the East where the Old Testament was written, names had great significance. Names were given to people, places, and things for the significance they had, or the significance desired by someone. The Bible teaches that the main significance of My many names is that each one gives further information about me.

My first name is God, or *Elohim*. My second name is LORD (all letters are capitalized) or *Jehovah*. And My third name is *Adonai*, or Master, or Lord (with only the first letter capitalized). Three names do not mean you are talking about different gods, but one God. You are not talking about different views of God. You are talking about one God who has revealed Himself through His different names, and you are talking about one God who reveals His different relationships to humans through His different names.

When referring to My strength, the name *Elohim* (God) is used. It occurs thirty-one times in Genesis 1 to reveal My creative power. When referring to My existing nature of My relationship with people, My name *Jehovah* (LORD) is used. My title *Adonai* (Lord) is used when referring to My authority over a person such as the relationship of Master to servant.

54 – I Am Elohim: Creator God

55 – I Am LORD: Jehovah, "I Am I Am"

56 – I Am Lord: Adonai, Master

57 – I Am Father

54

I AM ELOHIM, CREATOR GOD

The first time in the Bible I am identified; I am called *God*. As God, I am the all-powerful Creator of everything. "In the beginning God [Elohim] created the heavens and the earth" (Gen. 1:1).

Elohim comes from *El*, meaning "strong one" and *alah* meaning "to swear or bind with an oath." The term *Elohim* is used 2,500 times in the Bible to identify Me, the Creator God. This the name I am usually identified by the world.

God is a universal term for deity, used by almost all religions. My name, Elohim (God) is one of the three primary terms used to describe Me in the Bible. Elohim is the strong Creator God who is the Source of everything.

Names are important to people and their friends. When someone calls a friend by the wrong name or title, it probably means they are not as close as they think.

When people say, "God saved me," or "I know God," they are using an impersonal title for Me. Those who know Me and worship Me, call Me Father (John 4:23, 14:23-24).

All religions have a god. But those children who are saved will usually call Me LORD God when they say, "The LORD saved me." Or they talk about "knowing Me, the LORD." But when they pray, they call Me our Father in heaven.

The difference between God and the LORD may be very subtle to some, but those who know Me—the LORD—know the difference. The study of the word *Elohim* (God) in this chapter will form a basis for the study of the word *Jehovah* (LORD) in the next chapter.

WHO IS GOD?

There are many definitions of God. But I the God of the Bible am the Supreme Being, the Divine One whom you worship. Definitions must have a definitive term, such as "the man is a husband." From the Bible we can draw at least seven definitive terms used to describe Me the God of the universe.

Who is God?

1. I am life.
2. I am a person.
3. I am Spirit.
4. I am a self-existent being.
5. I am unity.
6. I am unchangeable.
7. I am unlimited in space and time.

I AM LIFE

When Joshua told his people, "You shall know that the living God is among you" (Josh. 3:10), he was describing Me by the term "life" or "living." Even young David recognized this definition when he spoke of Goliath defying "the living God" (1 Sam. 17:26). To call Me "Life" is more than describing Me as the One who created life, or as the Source of life. I am the essence or nature of life. The world may say that life is energy, power, or force. But the Bible says that I am the Life and Source behind them all. I am the living God who used My energy to create the world. It is My power—it is Me who hold atoms and molecules together, the smallest existence of life. The Bible expands this truth: "By Me all things consist" (Col. 1:17 ELT). *Pray: Lord, live in me and through me.*

I AM A PERSON

Whereas most of the religions in the world identify their deities by concepts such as a force or other kinds of impersonal beings, the Bible paints a higher picture of Me. I have intellect, emotion, and will, which are the elements of personality. In addition to this, I have self-awareness and self-determination. My personality is projected into human in what the Scripture calls "an image of God." Humanity mirrors Me when exercising their personality.

My personality is seen in My intelligence. I know (see Gen. 18:19; Exod. 3:7) and I have infinite wisdom (see Jeremiah 51:15). I have all the properties or essence of intelligence—thinking, remembrance, comparing.

Next, I have feelings or emotions, sometimes called "sensibility." I feel grief (see Gen. 6:6), kindness (see Ps. 103:8-13), empathy (see Exod.

3:7-8), anger (see Ps. 7:11), plus a whole array of other feelings including joy and anger.

Then I have a will, which is the volitional reflection of My personhood. I can make decisions and choose or direct My own actions. I am not bound by any force in the universe, for I am free to do, think, and decide as I choose.

Because I have given you an intellect in My own image, you can predict some of My actions. You know, for example, that I will always act in love. But you cannot coerce My actions, since I am perfectly free. No outside stimulus can make Me go against My will or choice. *Pray: I am humbled to be a person like You.*

I AM SPIRIT

In the New Testament, Jesus told the Samaritan woman, "God is Spirit; and those who worship Him must worship in spirit and truth" (John 4:24). Even though the King James Version uses the article "a" with spirit, I am not one Spirit among many spirits. The verse means I am Spirit by nature. As such, I do not have a physical body; I am an incorporeal Being. I am a real Being who has personality and life, but I do not live through a physical body.

Another way of saying this is that I am invisible. Some Bible references imply that people saw Me (see Gen. 32:30; Exod. 34:5-8; Num. 12:6-8; Deut. 34:10; Isa. 6:1). Actually, they did not see Me directly, but only My reflection. The only ones who have seen Me are those who saw Jesus Christ, "the image of the invisible God" (Col. 1:15). To say that I am Spirit is to say that people have not seen Me. One of the reasons the second commandment prohibits making idols or images is because I am not physical or material (see Exod. 20:4). I am Spirit, and I want people to worship Me in My true nature. *Pray: Lord receive my worship, but teach me to worship more and to worship deeper.*

I AM A SELF-EXISTENT, SELF-DIRECTING BEING

Even though this chapter is defining Me as *Elohim*, My second name or My other title "LORD" (*Jehovah*) indicates that I am self-existent. The name *Jehovah* comes from the verb "I am." When Moses prayed to Me at the burning bush (see Exod. 3:1-15), he asked Me to identify Myself. I answered by saying, "I AM WHO I AM" (Exod. 3:14). This is another expression for LORD or *Jehovah*. The phrase "I AM WHO I AM" actually means "the Self-Existent God." In essence, I, *Jehovah*, am saying, "I exist by Myself and for Myself." My existence is not dependent upon this world, humanity, or anything else. I am the One who depends upon only Myself. *Pray: Lord I know I exist, and because of that truth, I know You exist.*

I AM UNITY

The great *Shema* recited by obedient Jews is based on My nature: "Hear [Hebrew: *shema*] O Israel: The LORD our God, the LORD is one!" (Deut. 6:4). There can only be one God. To say that there are two supreme gods, or two creators is definitionally inconsistent. It is like describing a square circle—there is no such thing as a circle that is square. There can only be one Supreme being; if there were two, these forces would clash. My nature excludes all others, for no other one can do what I can do. This truth is taught in Scripture: "Thus saith the LORD the

King of Israel, and his redeemer the LORD of hosts; I am the first, and I am the last; and beside me there is no God" (Isa. 44:6 KJV). *Pray: Lord, help my personality come together, as Your personality is unity.*

I AM UNCHANGEABLE

Since I am perfect, I cannot become better; I am immutable—I cannot change in My essence. And since I am perfect, I cannot become corrupt and be less than God. The Bible states, "God is not a man, that he should lie; neither the son of man, that he should repent..." (Num. 23:19).

This does not mean that I cannot change My mind. The King James Version says that man became so wicked before the Flood that "it repented the LORD that he had made man" (Gen. 6:6). I also "repenteth" that I had made Saul king (1 Sam. 15:11 KJV). But a careful study of such passages reveals that man turned from Me in sinful rebellion. I did not change in My essence—rather, consistent with My unchanging nature, rather than blessing the people, I judged their sin. The real change was in humanity; and this called for a change in the way that I responded to people.

This is true today, I am still unchanged, even though My way of responding to your request depends on your response to Me. Obedience will bring reward, and disobedience will bring punishment. I do not change; men and women just move from one side of My nature to the other. The changing lifestyles of people cause My consistent reaction to appear to change, but the essential change is not in Me. I am unchangeable. *Pray: Lord, help me be unchangeable like You.*

I AM UNLIMITED IN SPACE AND TIME

In the beginning I created everything, including time and space. This means that I am LORD of time and space; I am not bound by My creation. The Bible says that it is I who "inhabits eternity" (Isa. 57:15)—a realm beyond time and space. Abraham recognized Me as "the Everlasting God" (Gen. 21:33). Moses observed that "even from everlasting to everlasting, You are God" (Ps. 90:2). The psalmist wrote, "But You are the same, and Your years will have no end" (Ps. 102:27).

What is time? Time is the measurement of events that appear in sequence. I existed before the first event—creation. I never had a beginning point, and I will continue without a terminal point. I will always exist.

What is space? Space is all of the area in which there is physical reality and being. Space is the distance between objects. But I am greater than space: "God, who made the world and everything in it, since He is Lord of heaven and earth, does not dwell in temples made with hands" (Acts 17:24).

Since time and space are the result of My creative acts, I am not limited by My creation. I am infinite in relationship to time (the sequence of events) and to space (the distance between objects). I am the only Being who exists without limitations.

If there were another God, then I *Elohim* would not be the self-existing, all-powerful, unlimited God. Since there cannot be two unlimited beings, there cannot be a God other than Me. For if there were another God, then neither God could be an unlimited God. My infinity and immensity are strong arguments for My sovereignty in the universe and in your life.

There is a clear command in the Bible, "Be still, and know that I am God [*Elohim*]..." (Ps. 46:10). You can seek Me and know Me through

My name, for My name reveals My nature (who I am) and My works (what I have done for you). You should remember, however, that as you are searching to know Me, I also am searching you and examining you. As David gave his son Solomon the plans for the temple, he said:

> *Know the God of your father, and serve Him with a perfect heart and with a willing mind: for the LORD searches all hearts, and understands all the imagination of their thoughts: if you seek Him, He will be found by you; but if you reject Him, He will reject you* (1 Chron. 28:9 ELT).

When you begin to know Me, you begin to learn yourself. "I created man in My own image, in My image created I him; male and female I created them" (Gen. 1:27 ELT). Therefore, the more you learn about Me, the more you learn about yourself. Because you are created in My image, subconsciously there is a desire to know Me, your Creator. But part of knowing yourself is realizing that this longing to know Me can never be realized completely.

When Jesus prayed the night before His death, He said, "And this is eternal life, that they may know You, the only true God, and Jesus Christ whom You have sent" (John 17:3). Those who know My Son Jesus receive eternal life. And those who are saved have learned of Me by faith: "But without faith it is impossible to please Him, for he who comes to God must believe that He is, and that He is a rewarder of those who diligently seek Him" (Heb. 11:6). *Pray: Lord, I pray with Jesus.*

YOUR TIME TO PRAY

God, I know You exist, thank You for creating me.
I am a descendent of Adam—one of Your creations.
Thank You for giving me physical life through my parents,
I receive my life from You and give my life back to You.
God, You are intellect, emotion, and will, and
I am a person, made in Your image and likeness.
I acknowledge Your eternal Personhood, and
Worship You for Your magnificent gift of life to me.
God, thank You for creating me with self-awareness and self-direction.
I give myself back to You.
You are my Creator-God, and my eternal LORD,
and my Lord and Master. I will serve You.
Amen.

I AM LORD— JEHOVAH, "I AM I AM"

> God replied to Moses, "I AM WHO I AM. Say this to the people of Israel: I AM has sent me to you." God also said to Moses, "Say this to the people of Israel: Yahweh, the God of your ancestors—the God of Abraham, the God of Isaac, and the God of Jacob—has sent me to you. This is my eternal name, my name to remember for all generations"
> —Exodus 3:14-15 NLT

A little boy sat down at his kindergarten desk and announced, "I'm going to color a picture of God."

"But no one knows what God looks like," responded his teacher.

"They will when I get finished," the boy said, with childlike confidence.

This little boy is just like many who think their God is what they define or describe Him to be. Obviously, the little boy and public opinion is wrong. I am who I am, and no human or anything else can change Me.

I reveal different names to people in their crises. My name *Jehovah* (LORD) is one of the earliest of My names that I revealed to Moses when he approached Me at the burning bush. I revealed My name to give people an indication of who I am, and what I am like.

My name LORD (*Jehovah*) is the second name used for Me in the Old Testament. My name "God" (*Elohim*), the universally recognized name for deity, is found in the first verse of the Bible, "In the beginning God created the heavens and the earth" (Gen. 1:1). But My second name, "LORD," is the one used most often in Scripture, occurring 6,823 times in the Old Testament, and to modern Jews, it was their primary name for Me.

The word *Jehovah* or *Yahweh*—can be pronounced either way. My name "LORD" comes from the Hebrew verb *hayah*, which signifies "to be" or "to become." (Remember that it is spelled with upper case capitals—LORD—to distinguish it from Lord, meaning *Adonai* or Master. When translated in the first person, it becomes "I am" said twice. Hence, when Moses anticipated that the Israelites would ask about My name, I said to tell them, "I AM WHO I AM" (Exod. 3:14). Then I the LORD said, "Thus you shall say to the children of Israel, "I AM has sent me to you" (Exod. 3:14).

My name "LORD," therefore, points to their God who is continuously revealing Himself as "the Self-Existing One." I am who I say I am; therefore, I am the eternal One. Some interpret My name "LORD" as containing two truths in one name. The first meaning of LORD is "the One who exists in Himself," and the second is "the One who reveals Himself."

My name "LORD" goes beyond the meaning of My first name: "God" (*Elohim*), "the strong Creator." I *Elohim* created the world in Genesis 1:1, but in Genesis 2:4, I *Elohim* am identified as *Jehovah* ("LORD God"): "This is the history of the heavens and the earth when they were created, in the day that the LORD God made the earth and the heavens."

Many think My second name, "LORD," is perhaps My favorite name. I told Moses, "I appeared unto Abraham, unto Isaac, and unto Jacob, by the name of God Almighty [*El Shaddai*], but by My name JEHOVAH was I not known to them" (Exod. 6:3 KJV). Throughout Scripture, I constantly refer to Myself by the name "LORD," seldom by the name "God." Why do I do this? Perhaps because there are so many gods; every false religion has its substitute god. But there is only one God named LORD who is the Self-Existing One.

The uncertainty about how to pronounce My name *Jehovah* comes because there were no vowels in the original Hebrew. There were only the consonants that are transliterated into English as JHVH or YHWH. The vowels were developed later from Hebrew pronunciation marks. Out of reverence for My name, LORD, the rabbis in Old Testament Judaism would not write it or pronounce it, perhaps because of the verse, "Holy and reverent is My name" (Ps. 111:9 ELT). Hence, the way they pronounced YHWH became obscure. But many times, they would write and pronounce My name God, *Elohim*.

My name "LORD" (*Jehovah*) is used in relationship to people, while My name "God" is used primarily in references to nature or My creation. After I *Elohim* created the world, the name "LORD" was added because I the strong Creator wanted to relate to those I created. First, I was identified: "The LORD God had not caused it to rain upon the earth" (Gen. 2:5 KJV). Next you find, "I the LORD God planted a garden eastward in Eden" (Gen. 2:8 KJV). Man was given the task of tending the garden.

Finally, "The LORD God said, It is not good that the man should be alone" (Gen. 2:18 KJV). As a result of seeing the loneliness of man, "The LORD God caused a deep sleep to fall upon Adam and he slept: and he took one of his ribs...and the rib, which the LORD God had taken from man, made he a woman..." (Gen. 2:21-22 KJV). Hence, I the LORD God am concerned about man's relationship to woman and about both man and woman's relationships to Me.

When the element of evil is introduced into the story, then it broke the relationship between Me and My created ones. "Now the serpent was more cunning than any beast of the field which the LORD God had made" (Gen. 3:1). Because they did not resist the serpent's temptation, Adam and Eve fell into sin. But I, the redemptive LORD came seeking them: "They heard the voice of the LORD God walking in the garden in the cool of the day" (Gen. 3:8 KJV). I the LORD did not come to judge them but ultimately to save them. I asked a question, "What is this that you have done?" (Gen. 3:13).

I warned the serpent that the seed of woman would bruise its head (Gen. 3:15). That is the *protoevangelium*—the first hint of the gospel, the good news that Jesus Christ, born of woman, would conquer evil and be the means of salvation. But I the LORD was not finished. "Also for Adam and his wife the LORD God made tunics of skins, and clothed them" (Gen. 3:21). In this act, I the LORD obviously had to take the life of an animal, you presume a lamb. This animal became a foreshadow of all of the lambs that would be sacrificed for the sins of humanity until the ultimate Lamb—Jesus Christ—took away the sin of the world (see John 1:29). Hence, early in the book of Genesis, My name "LORD" reflects a redemptive relationship with humankind.

In the last chapter, I God (*Elohim*) was defined under the question, "Who is God?" In this chapter, I *Jehovah* am described in answer to the question, "What is the LORD like?" The last chapter gave a definition of Me, while here you focus on a description of the LORD. *Pray: Lord, help me know You better and worship You deeper.*

I have traditionally been described by My attributes. An attribute reflects what comes from My nature. Just as the rays from the sun give meaning to the sun and reflect its nature, so too My attributes reflect My nature. People know what the sun is like because of its rays. In much the same way, you can know something of what I the LORD am like from My attributes. *Pray: Lord, I will look beyond Your attributes to know You intimately.*

Six attributes were discussed in this book. The first three are absolute or moral attributes because they deal with My moral qualities that are beyond comparison with human attributes: 1) I the LORD am holy; 2) I am love; and 3) I am good. The second three are comparative or non-moral attributes because they deal with natural attributes that to some extent can be compared with human qualities.

Hence, I the LORD am: 1) omniscient or all-knowing; 2) omnipresent or present everywhere; and 3) omnipotent or all-powerful. The hymn writer Charles Wesley spoke of My attributes as "glorious all and numberless." Since I the LORD am the Self-Existing One who continuously reveals Myself, I have many attributes of which you are not yet aware. Charles Wesley was right; I have attributes that are numberless. I will continue to reveal Myself throughout all eternity, and you will continue to learn more about Me. *Pray: Yes Lord, continue revealing Yourself to me.*

YOUR TIME TO PRAY

Lord, when I ask who You are, You answer, "I Am."
Forgive me for ignorantly asking the question.
Lord, You satisfy me saying, "I am the Lord of life.
You guide my life saying, "I am the Light."
Lord, You opened heaven saying, "I am the Door."
You offered me protection saying, "I am the Good Shepherd."
Lord, You offered me eternity saying, "I am Resurrection and Life."
You offered me intimacy, saying, "I am the Vine, you are the branches."
Amen.

56

I AM LORD—
ADONAI, MASTER

> *But Abram said, "Lord GOD, [Adonai, Elohim] what will You give me, seeing I go childless...."* —Genesis 15:2

The first time the word *Adonai* "Master" is used in Scripture as one of My names reveals something about My relationship to humans. Abraham had been in the Promised Land for ten years. I had promised Abraham the land and a son as his great inheritance. But Abraham and Sarah were past the age of bearing children. After ten years it was only natural that Abraham was growing restless and impatient. He prayed to Me calling Me his Master, "Lord GOD [*Adonai Jehovah*], what will You give me, seeing I go childless?" (Gen. 15:2). Notice the "L" in My name Lord is capitalized, but the remaining letters are not.

In this reference, Abraham had a burden for two things. First, he wanted an offspring—a son. Second, he wanted the inheritance that had been promised him. Perhaps Abraham realized that the inheritance was tied to the son. After ten years Abraham did not have either a son or the Promised Land. Inasmuch as Abraham had a servant-Master relationship to Me, it is only natural that he addressed Me using the names *Adonai* ("Master") and *Jehovah* ("the Covenant-Keeping God").

Again, Abraham prayed, "Lord GOD [*Adonai Jehovah*], how shall I know that I will inherit it?" (Gen. 15:8). I had promised him that I would take care of him. Now Abraham wanted some assurance.

Names and titles are important because they open doors. Wrong use of names reveals your ignorance and says you don't know what you are doing or where you are going. Using wrong names and titles shuts doors because it shows that you are not worthy of an opportunity.

You have seen that the Bible uses different names for Me to reflect My different roles and functions. When you use My name correctly in prayer, it shows you respect Me and know how to approach Me. I would not refuse to hear your prayers because you used an inappropriate title— but your wrong use may reflect your spiritual immaturity. It shows you have not taken time to get to know Me, your Master. Since My name is *Adonai* (Master), you should approach Me properly using that name.

*Adon*ai comes from the Hebrew word *adon*, a word used to describe either a master who owns servants or a husband in his relationship to his wife, although it does not imply that husbands own wives. *Adonai* is a plural form implying My Trinity nature, just as *Elohim* is also plural, implying My Trinity nature. Both are an Old Testament reference to Father, Son, and Holy Spirit.

My name *Adonai* is translated in Scripture as Lord (only the first letter capitalized) and it occurs 340 times in the Hebrew Old Testament. However, the rabbis eventually began using My name *Adonai* as a substitute for My name *Jehovah;* because *Jehovah* was holy, they were not even to speak or write My personal name. On many occasions when copying the Scriptures, they substituted My name *Adonai* for *Jehovah*. Then to make sure people knew that the terms were substituted, they prepared a parallel manual called the *Sopherim*, which listed the 140 places in the Scriptures where *Adonai* had been substituted for *Jehovah*.

My name *Adonai* expresses a personal relationship between the Master and His servant. Hence it is a term that symbolizes My relationship with My people. The relationship not only emphasizes ownership but implies a serving relationship. There must be a oneness between you and Me if we are to enjoy a "trust relationship." Hence, *Adonai* has a twofold meaning. Master means relationship and Lordship means ownership.

The relationship between master and servant does not begin with the servant but with the master, who must do two things. First, he must provide for the needs of his servants providing a place to sleep, food, clothing, and the basic necessities. Second, the master must provide direction, training, and accountability for the service of the servants.

Hence, the term *Adonai* puts more responsibility on Me than on My people. In a sense, a master serves the servants, for when a person is a servant, he or she looks to the master for direction, protection, and care. *Pray: You Adonai Lord are my Maker, let me serve You.*

YOUR MASTER-SERVANT RELATIONSHIP

The term *Adonai* (Master) explains the very heart of Christianity—the relationship between Me and the believer. Christians are different from nonbelievers because they relate to Me; the unsaved in the world deny that relationship. *Pray: Lord, I cherish our Master-servant relationship.*

What does the name *Adonai* (Master) assure for you as a believer? First, it assures you that I your God and Master have the resources and ability to take care of you. Thus, as a Christian servant, you trust Me for these things. Second, it implies that help is available to carry out your Christian duty as a servant. My help is seen in giving you spiritual gifts, leading you, supplying spiritual power and sending the Holy Spirit to minister through you. Finally, as My servant, you have the privilege of calling upon our relationship to get help when needed.

Moses also had a servant-Master relationship with Me. He felt inadequate when I commissioned him to go to Pharaoh to demand the release of My people from bondage. Moses only had My rod against the power of the Egyptian nation. After offering several excuses to Me, he finally prayed, "O my Lord [*Adonai*], I am not eloquent" (Exod. 4:10). Moses had a speech impediment. Yet he knew he must speak to Pharaoh, king of the strongest nation on earth. So, My servant Moses came to Me to ask for help. It was only natural that he used the title *Adonai*, Master.

Joshua led Israel across the Jordan River into battle against Jericho. Because I was with him, Joshua experienced a great victory (see Josh. 6). Shortly thereafter, he allowed only a few of his men to go to battle against Ai. But there was sin in Israel's camp, and My people were defeated. Joshua approached Me in prayer (Josh. 7:1-6). He came as a servant reminding Me his Master that he needed direction and power to conquer the Promised Land. Therefore, in this context it is only natural that Joshua used My title *Adonai*, Master. He prayed, "O Lord [Master, *Adonai*], what shall I say when Israel turns its back before its enemies?" (Josh. 7:8). The prayer of Joshua is based on his servant relationship with Me. Obviously, I answered by pointing out the sin, giving them a strategy and finally leading them to victory in battle (see Josh. 7:10-8:28).

Gideon was a young man who was fearful of the raiding Midianites who swept through the Promised Land destroying the Israelites' cattle and crops (see Judg. 6:1-6). I the Lord came to Gideon when he was hiding in the valley in a winepress, threshing his grain. As background, only those who were fearful and hiding would have attempted to thresh grain in a valley. Usually the threshing floor was on the highest elevated peak, unobstructed so that the wind could blow away the chaff. I came to Gideon and said, "The LORD is with you, you mighty man of valor!" (Judg. 6:12). This may have been an attempt to compliment or affirm Gideon, who was obviously an introvert with a self-acceptance problem. "And Gideon said unto him, Oh my Lord [Master, *Adonai*], if the LORD be with us, why then is all this befallen us?" (Judg. 6:13 KJV).

I AM Lord—Adonai, Master

Gideon prayed to Me in a servant-Master relationship. He recognized that I the Master could give him guidance and power. I the Lord promised Gideon was going to have a great victory, saying, "Go in this might of your, and you shall save Israel from the hand of the Midianites. Have not I sent you?" (Judg. 6:14). But Gideon still wanted more answers from Me, *Adonai* Master. He prayed, "Oh my Lord [Master, *Adonai*], how can I save Israel?" (Judg. 6:15). Based on this prayer, I gave Gideon the direction for his victory.

Others in Scripture have claimed the same relationship between servant and Master in their service to Me. When Manoah, who was childless, received word of My promise of a son, she prayed to Me the Master (*Adonai*, see Judg. 13:8). When Samson prayed to defeat the Philistines, he called upon Me in his servant-Master relationship (see Judg. 16:28). When David prayed to build a temple, he assumed a servant-Master relationship. Since he knew that I would give his son Solomon the resources and wisdom to build the temple, David prayed as My servant, knowing that I *Adonai* would supply (see 2 Sam. 7:18).

The psalmist connects the names *Jehovah* and *Adonai* in an outburst of praise in Psalm 8:1: "O LORD [*Jehovah*], our Lord, [Master, *Adonai*], how excellent is Your name in all the earth...!" *Pray: I join their praise.*

When Isaiah was praying in the temple, he saw Me the Lord (*Adonai*) high and exalted, sitting on the throne (Isa. 6:1). Isaiah's ruler and friend, King Uzziah, had died of leprosy. Some might assume that Isaiah's personal world had collapsed. What he needed was a vision of Me his Master, I the Lord (*Adonai*) sitting on the throne. But he also saw Me as LORD *Jehovah*. For the angels around the throne cried, "Holy, holy, holy, is the LORD [*Jehovah*] of hosts" (Isa. 6:3).

When Isaiah was called to serve Me, he was a proud, young diplomat-bureaucrat who worked for the king. He needed to be broken to enter into a Master-servant relationship with Me. Therefore, I showed Isaiah his sin and he cried, "Woe is me!" (Isa. 6:5).

The Old Testament Hebrew *Adonai* (Master) is the counterpart for the Greek New Testament *Kurios* (Lord). Jesus Christ is the Christian's Lord and Master. He said, "Ye call me Master and Lord: and ye say well; for so I am" (John 13:13 KJV).

My title *Adonai* gives you the believer the privilege of having Me as your Master who will care for you, supply your needs, and give you direction in life. As a Christian you do not have to be anxious about supplying your "daily bread" (Matt. 6:11)—that is the Master's responsibility. You do not have to fret over what job you should do or where you should serve—there is a "Master" plan for your life (see Rom. 12:1-2). You do not have to be concerned about whether you can do the things that I have for you to do—I promised the gifts of the Holy Spirit to enable you to serve Me (see 1 Cor. 12:3-8). *Pray: Master, I yield to You, show me how to serve You.*

Christians should recognize Jesus as Lord and submit to that relationship. When they do that, they will hear the words, "Well done, good and faithful servant; you were faithful over a few things.... Enter into the joy of your lord" (Matt. 25:21).

YOUR TIME TO PRAY

I bow to You Elohim God, You are my Creator,
I am only Your creation; I want to serve You today.
I worship You LORD, You are my personal Lord,
Come indwell me today and show Your greatness
I submit to You Lord, my Master who owns my life,
Show me how to serve You today,
Guide me in Your ministry today,
Use me as I do Your will today,
Fill me will power as I minister for You today.
Amen.

57

I AM FATHER

> *Our Father in heaven....* —Matthew 6:9
> *I thank You, Father, Lord of heaven and earth....*
> —Luke 10:21
> *God and Father of all....* —Ephesians 4:6

If you have ever seen a person bow down to a piece of stone or carved idol, you are watching a relationship—strained and fearful. What runs through the mind of a lost person who curses with the name of God—you hear anger or revenge or rage. God is not One who makes them happy or hopeful; and surely they don't feel an intimate relationship with Me. They are usually angry at their god.

But a Christian believer thinks of Me differently. An earthly father gives physical life to his children; they have their father's blood and nature. When you believe on Jesus and are forgiven by His death, you are born again into My family (John 3:3-7), and you are My child, and you along with other believers call Me "Abba [daddy], Father" (Rom. 8:14-16). This is a personal, intimate relationship.

I have a protective relationship with My children. Jesus said that earthly fathers "know how to give good gifts to your children, how much more swill your heavenly Father give..." (Luke 11:13). It is a biblical fact that I your heavenly Father loves My children (John 3:16) and provide for them.

There is another level of My care for you and all My children. I protect My children, "...they shall never perish, neither shall anyone snatch them out of My hand" (John 10:28). The greatest protection of all is your eternal security that you will live forever with Me your Father in heaven. Jesus promised, "There is more than enough room in my Father's home. ...I will come and get you, so that you will always be with me where I am" (John 14:1-3 NLT).

The next level of My care for My children is their access to Me. Think of a small child crawling up into the lap of their father to cuddle for enjoyment, or just sitting there for protection from the cares and worries of life. The apostle John offers you that fellowship with Me and My Son Jesus Christ when he writes, "that you also may have fellowship...with the Father and with His Son Jesus Christ" (1 John 1:3). *Pray: Yes, You are my heavenly Father and I am Your child.*

I your Father want all My children to enjoy My presence, but there is another side to that relationship. I want all My children to grow in grace and be conformed to the likeness of My Son (Rom. 8:29). So, I will work all thing together for good (Rom. 8:28), but I also must teach My children and correct My children and even discipline My children (Heb. 12:5-8). But like most children, they do not enjoy correction, or even the punishment from their heavenly Father. So, remember, "He who did not spare His own Son...how shall He not with Him also freely give us all things?" (Rom. 8:32). *Pray: Father, I trust You.*

That takes us to another level of intimacy. Because you are My child, you are My heir, "...heirs of God and joint heirs with Christ..." (Rom. 8:17). All the benefits I promised to all My children will one day be yours—because you are family, you are My child. *Pray: Father, thank You.*

YOUR TIME TO PRAY

LORD, You are the eternal "I Am" and I worship
Your majestic power and glory.
God, You are the Creator who sculptured me in Your image.
Lord, You are my Master, tell me where to go and what to do.
Father, You seek my worship and I bow to You.
You invite me to know You intimately.
So, I will get close to You and say, "I love You!"
Amen.

Section H

LEARNING MY TRINITARIAN NATURE

The teaching of one God in three Persons has challenged Christians throughout the ages to understand this glorious revelation of mystery. The Father, Son, and Holy Spirit are each distinguishable from each other, yet the nature and attributes of each are possessed by the other two. The Trinity is a description of God in unity yet existing in three eternal Persons. The members of the Trinity are equal in nature, distinct in Person, yet submissive in duties.

As Son, Jesus is eternally begotten by the Father, so Jesus is submissive to do the work of the Father, yet equal in nature to Him: "...The LORD has said to Me, "You are My Son, today I have begotten You" (Ps. 2:7). Then the Son sends the Holy Spirit: "The Comforter...I will send unto you from the Father..." (John 15:26 KJV). Later Jesus prayed to the Father, saying, "...I have finished the work which You have given Me to do" (John 17:4). The Father is the source of authority, the Son is the channel, and the Holy Spirit is the agent whereby authority is exercised.

The oldest existing identification of the Trinity is the *Athanasian Creed* written about AD 250: "We worship one God, in Trinity, and

Trinity in unity, neither confounding the persons, nor dividing the substance."

Nearly two centuries ago, John Dick put the same truth this way: "While there is only one divine nature, there are three subsistence, or persons, called the Father, the Son, and the Holy Ghost, who possess, not a similar, but the same numerical essence, and the distinction between them is not merely nominal, but real."

Theological definition: I am Father, Son, and Holy Spirit, equal in nature, separate in Person, and submissive in ministry.

| 58 – I Am Trinity, Three in One

58

I AM TRINITY—
THREE IN ONE

> *The grace of My Son, the Lord Jesus Christ, and My love from your heavenly Father, and the communion of the Holy Spirit, be with you all, amen.* —2 Corinthians 13:14 ELT

A human like Elmer Towns can be three different personalities in one day. As an author, he studies in the morning, writing his notes or an article from the things he discovered in his research. Then he takes his children and grandchildren out to lunch, taking the smaller ones to the dollar store and telling them he will buy them anything they want. In this playful role, he is a grandparent. Later for exercise he plays nine holes as a golfer. Author, grandparent, and golfer – all in one day.

Yet this is a poor illustration of the Trinity, of Me the Father, Me the Son the Lord Jesus Christ, and of Me the Holy Spirit. Elmer Towns is only one person *doing* three things. In the Trinity, We are three distinct and separate persons, but at the same time We are One. As stated in the introduction of Section H, the Athanasian Creed is one of the oldest creeds of the Christian faith, describes Our Trinity: "We worship one God in Trinity, and Trinity in unity; neither confounding the persons, nor dividing the substance." This teaches the Trinity is Father, Son, and Holy Spirit, three distinct persons who exist together in unity. Each member of the Trinity is totally God with submissive roles to one another.

Each member of the Trinity is fully God existing in unity, but separate in person, equal in nature, and submissive to one another in ministry.

How are we submissive to each other? The Father sent His only begotten Son (see Ps. 2:7), and the Father and Son (see John 15:26) sent the Holy Spirit to work and minister in and through believers and in the world.

You can also try to understand My triune nature by thinking about the people it takes to build a house. The Father is the architect-engineer who plans the house design. The Son is the contractor who goes to the site (the earth) to do the work of construction. The Holy Spirit is the worker who actually does the physical construction work. Each needs the other and all three must work together in unison for the project to be complete. This is a good illustration of construction, but it has many limitations in describing Our duties and nature.

Sometimes it is easier to understand the Trinity by looking at what the Trinity is not. The Trinity is not three Gods (tritheism). Christians are monotheists, meaning they believe in one God. "Hear, O Israel: The LORD our God, the LORD is one!" (Deut. 6:4). So, they don't believe in three Gods.

Also, the Trinity is not three different manifestations of one God. This is *modalism* that teaches the Old Testament Father *becomes* the Son, who in turn *becomes* the Holy Spirit. The basic error of modalism is it denies the distinctiveness of each Person of the Godhead, and it denies the eternality of each three Persons. God is not sometimes the Father, sometimes the Son, and sometimes the Holy Spirit. I am all three, all the time.

Also, the Son and the Holy Spirit are not mere attributes or influences of the Father. The Bible teaches Jesus was God. "In the beginning

I Am Trinity—Three in One

was the Word, and the Word was with God, and the Word was God" (John 1:1). Then it says, "The Word became flesh..." (John 1:14), meaning Jesus the Word became a human body. So, the Son is not just a characteristic of God; He is a Person and He is God.

A number of examples of My triune nature can be found in the Bible. The way I talked with Myself in Scripture reflects the Trinity. There was a plurality among the Godhead in the beginning when I said, "Let *Us* make man in *Our* image..." (Gen. 1:26). When the Godhead appeared to Isaiah, I said, "Who will go for *Us?*" (Isa. 6:8).

Another clear example of the Trinity can be seen in the baptism of Jesus recorded in Matthew. After Jesus the God-Man was baptized in the Jordan River, the Father from heaven said, "This is My beloved Son, in whom I am well pleased," and the Holy Spirit in the form of a dove descends on Jesus (Matt. 3:16-17). All three Persons of God––Father, Son, and Holy Spirit were present for the event. *Pray: Lord, I was not present for that magnificent event, but I read it in the Scriptures. Then I bow in worship for its eternal significance.*

The early church also worshipped in a Trinitarian formula. "The grace of our Lord Jesus Christ, and the love of God the Father, and the communion of the Holy Spirit be with you all" (2 Cor. 13:14 ELT).

As further proof, look at the way Jesus instructed how to baptize a new convert, "In the name of the Father and of the Son and of the Holy Spirit" (Matt. 28:19).

Finally, one of the strongest proofs of the Trinity is that the Bible reveals that each member of the Trinity possesses the same attributes and tasks of the other members.

ATTRIBUTES OF THE TRINITY

ATTRIBUTES	FATHER	SON	HOLY SPIRIT
Omnipresence	Jer. 23:24	Matt. 28:20	Ps. 139:7-12
Omnipotence	Rom. 1:16	Matt. 28:18	Rom. 15:19
Omniscience	Rom. 11:33	John 21:17	John 14:26
Immutability	Mal. 3:6	Heb. 13:8	Hag. 2:5
Eternality	Ps. 90:2	John 1:1	Heb. 9:14
Holiness	Lev. 19:2	Heb. 4:15	name "Holy"
Love	1 John 3:1	Matt. 9:36	name "Holy"

THE WORK OF THE TRINITY

WORK	FATHER	SON	HOLY SPIRIT
Creation of world	Ps. 102:25	John 1:3	Gen. 1:2
Creation of man	Gen. 2:7	Col. 1:16	Job 33:4
Death of Christ	Isa. 53:10	John 10:18	Heb. 9:14
Resurrection of Christ	Acts 2:32	John 2:19	1 Pet. 3:18
Inspiration	Heb. 1:1-2	1 Pet. 1:10-11	2 Pet. 1:21
Indwelling of believers	Eph. 4:6	Col. 1:7	1 Cor. 6:19
Authority of ministry	2 Cor. 3:4-6	1 Tim. 1:12	Acts 20:28
Security of believer	John 10:29	Phil. 1:6	Eph. 1:13-14

Christians believe in Me—one God in three Persons—Father, Son, and Holy Spirit. Each member of the Trinity is God and each member works in your life today. *Pray: Lord, I want You to work as Father, Son, and Holy Spirit in my life today.*

I want you to worship Me as you worship each member of the Godhead, who is worthy of worship and deserving of obedience. Each reveals themselves in Scripture and expect you to respond accordingly. *Pray: Lord, I love, worship, and obey You, the Triune God.*

YOUR TIME TO PRAY

Lord, I worship You, Father, Son, and Holy Spirit,
I cry holy, holy, holy to all Three.
You are Three in One, eternal God.
Lord, early in the morning I will come to You,
Praying for Your blessing on my life
And waiting for Your intimate presence.
Lord, I worship You Father for Your continuous love and mercy,
I praise You Jesus for eternal salvation,
I thank You Holy Spirit for powerfully working in my life.
Amen.

AFTERWORD

When you begin to describe God with the characteristics of humans, be careful you don't belittle God, or minimize God and try to make the eternal God who is almighty and holy like yourself. Beware!

> *"...You thought that I was altogether like you..."* (Ps. 50:21 NKJV).

In trying to make God more understandable to your thinking, you might do the opposite of what you want. Rather than making Him greater, you may shrink Him down to your perspective. Remember David said, "O magnify the Lord with me, and let us exalt His name together" (Ps. 34:3). Even the virgin Mary when she considered carrying the human embryo of Jesus in her womb prayed, "My soul magnifies the Lord" (Luke 1:46). *Pray: Lord, forgive me for every time I didn't accept the magnitude of Your greatness.*

The true idea of God can never be measured or compared to human characteristics. God has described Himself in human symbols or as having human actions, so we can understand, distinguish, and interpret what He is doing in the world and in us. As mentioned previously, these descriptions are called anthromorphisms—projections into the characteristics of humans. Remember, man was created in the image of God (Gen. 2:7). Therefore, the opposite is true. We are like God, not He like us.

It is only natural for humans to think there is a psychological or physiological likeness between God and us. Look at the heathen who have no basis for understanding God or describing how He reacts to them. They carve idols of wood, stone, or other substances thinking God is like the human they carve. They bow down to worship their idols. But worse than that, they bring sacrifices to their idols.

I watched it happen with my own eyes. I was with twenty-three students and leaders from Liberty University ministering in all the refugee camps along the Mekong River in Thailand, December 1978. Our van broke down and we were stuck for six hours. We sat on a balcony in a restaurant overlooking the Mekong River. There was an idol on the railing next to us. At noon, a waitress offered a plate of food to the idol, then bowed and was quiet. I think she was praying to the spirit of the idol. She did this when we first arrived, but a couple of hours later she carried the food away. She did it again four hours later. None of us could speak her language. Our interpreter was not with us, so we could not witness to her. I will always remember the complete devotion on her face as she offered her sacrifice to an idol.

So, go beyond the human term or physical attribute you attribute to God. He is the eternal God who existed in eternity, He has no beginning. You cannot think of Him in physical symbols or as one with limits. He is limitless. You cannot contain the One who is omnipresent—everywhere present at the same time. You cannot resist His power, the One who is omnipotent, who has all energy to do anything within His desire, nature, and existence. *Pray: Lord, teach me to always accept You as You are...and worship.*

So, God is not like us—we humans are like Him. All the human functions we perform or respond to are the functions of God. However, God does these functions without bodily parts.

Afterword

You cannot say God understands, because to us the process of understanding suggests investigation, research, comparing, and coming to a conclusion. No, don't say God has come to understand; it is proper to say God knows. He knows from the past, He knows what will happen in the future, God eternally knows everything without effort, recall, or consideration. Because God is, God knows everything actual and potential.

Let's examine one of the human characteristics and/or functions that we project with God. God has breath, like we have breath. Job said, "By the breath of his nostrils" (Job 4:9 KJV). If God had a nose, what would it look like? Then another question, "Does God have to breathe as we humans have to breathe to stay alive? If so, what would happen if God stopped breathing?" Job said at another place, "The spirit of God is in my nostrils" (Job 27:3 KJV). Job understood his breath came from God.

Moses wrote of God's actions in the beginning: "The LORD God formed man of the dust of the ground, and breathed into his nostrils the breath of life; and man became a living soul" (Gen. 2:7 KJV). So, our human breath is an extension of God's breath (life) that He blew into Adam's nose and lungs. Therefore, through the process of human reproduction, I have breath (life) that I got from my parents. This process can be traced all the way back to Adam...then to God.

The body that God sculptured out of red clay from the bank of the Euphrates River was in the mind of God before He sculptured the wet red clay. All the physical functions projected into God in this book were in His mind long before creation. *Pray: Lord, I believe!*

God the Father knew He would send His Son to redeem humans before "the foundation of the earth" (1 Peter 1:19-20). Our physical limits and functions were ordered for us because it followed the pattern that was created for Jesus. Christ said to the Father, "...a body You have prepared for Me'" (Heb. 10:5).

YOUR TIME TO PRAY

*LORD, forgive me for trying to understand You in human ways,
You are the eternal God of the ages. You are Almighty God.
Lord, forgive me when I explain You in terms that don't magnify You.
You are enthroned in majesty and enshrouded in mystery.
LORD, I see You in the pages of Scripture and know You;
I feel Your presence in meditation and prayer and believe You.
Lord, I come to You for assurance and guidance, and You give it.
I trust You with my inevitable death and coming future life in heaven.
Amen.*

ABOUT ELMER TOWNS

Dr. Elmer L. Towns is Dean Emeritus of the School of Religion and Theological Seminary at Liberty University, which he cofounded in 1971. He continues to teach the Pastor's Bible Class at Thomas Road Baptist Church each Sunday, which is televised on a local network and Angel One.

Experience a personal revival!

Spirit-empowered content from today's top Christian authors delivered directly to your inbox.

Join today!
lovetoreadclub.com

Inspiring Articles
Powerful Video Teaching
Resources for Revival

Get all of this and so much more, e-mailed to you twice weekly!

LOVE TO READ CLUB
by **D** DESTINY IMAGE